Clarity, Charm and Thoroughness

The greatest challenge of Western medicine is to educate and motivate patients to adopt a healthier lifestyle. *Dynamic Health* is doing exactly that—with clarity, charm and thoroughness.

—WILLIAM CASTELLI, MD
Former Director, Framingham Heart Study

Extend Your Life

These are important concepts that, when internalized, will do more to improve your health and extend your life than all the technological wonders of modern medicine.

—JOHN MCDOUGALL, MD
Internist and Author
McDougall's Medicine and Other Bestsellers

On the Cutting Edge

The authors are totally reliable and on the cutting edge of lifestyle medicine.

—NEAL BARNARD, MD
President, Physicians Committee
for Responsible Medicine

No One Can Read and Remain the Same

The authors have been in the forefront of preventive medicine since long before it was fashionable. They confront health questions and anxieties with compelling evidence and grace. No one can read even a few of these chapters and remain the same.

—HERBERT E. DOUGLASS, ThD
Former President, Weimar Institute

The Most Practical Key

This may be the most practical key to a better lifestyle that many of us have ever found.

—DAN MATTHEWS
Former Executive Producer/Host, *Lifestyle* Magazine

Dynamic HEALTH

HANS DIEHL, DrHSc
AND AILEEN LUDINGTON, MD

SILOAM
A STRANG COMPANY

DYNAMIC HEALTH by Hans Diehl, DrHSc, MPH, FACN and Aileen Ludington, MD
Published by Siloam
A Strang Company
600 Rinehart Road
Lake Mary, Florida 32746
www.siloam.com

Unless otherwise noted, all Scripture quotations are from the King James Version of the Bible.

Scripture quotations marked NIV are from the Holy Bible, New International Version. Copyright © 1973, 1978, 1984, International Bible Society. Used by permission.

Scripture quotations marked NKJV are from the New King James Version of the Bible. Copyright © 1979, 1980, 1982 by Thomas Nelson, Inc., publishers. Used by permission.

Cover design by Judith McKittrick
Interior design by Sallie Traynor

This book is not intended to provide medical advice or to take the place of medical advice and treatment from your personal physician. Readers are advised to consult their own doctors or other qualified health professionals regarding the treatment of their medical problems. Neither the publisher nor the author takes any responsibility for any possible consequences from any treatment, action or preparation to any person reading or following the information in this book. If readers are taking prescription medications, they should consult with their physicians and not take themselves off of medicines to start supplementation without the proper supervision of a physician.

NEWSTART *is a registered trademark of the Weimar Lifestyle Program. NEWSTART is an acronym based on eight health principles: Nutrition, Exercise, Water, Sunshine, Temperance, Air, Rest and Trust. Used by permission of Weimar Institute, Weimar, California 95736.*

Library of Congress Cataloging-in-Publication Data

Diehl, Hans, 1946-
  Dynamic health / Hans Diehl and Aileen Ludington.
    p. cm.
  ISBN 1-59185-231-5 (pbk.)
 1. Health. 2. Self-care, Health. 3. Nutrition. I. Ludington, Aileen, 1924- II. Title.
RA776 .D515 2003
613--dc22

                              2003015590

03 04 05 06 07 — 8 7 6 5 4 3 2 1
Printed in the United States of America

About the Authors

Hans Diehl, DrHSc, MPH, FACN

As a National Institutes of Health–sponsored research fellow in cardiovascular epidemiology at Loma Linda University, Dr. Diehl evaluated the impact of the Pritikin Longevity Center, where he served as director of the Research and Health Education program.

As a postdoctoral scholar at the School of Public Health at the University of California at Los Angeles, he contributed to the establishment of the UCLA Center for Health Enhancement. He holds a doctorate in health science with emphasis on lifestyle medicine and has a master's degree in public health nutrition from Loma Linda University.

Dr. Diehl is the founder and director of the Lifestyle Medicine Institute in Loma Linda, California. He is editor of *Lifeline Health Letter,* a best-selling author and the founder of the CHIP (Coronary Health Improvement Project) Program. He has demonstrated and published results showing that many hypertensives, diabetics and heart disease patients can normalize their disease and become drug-free within weeks by simplifying their customary rich Western diet.

Dr. Diehl travels widely as a seminar leader and appears frequently on TV and radio.

Aileen Ludington, MD

Dr. Ludington, a graduate of Loma Linda University, is a board-certified physician with twenty-five years of practice experience. Her lifelong interest in health education eventually led to a staff appointment at Weimar Institute's residential NEWSTART Lifestyle Center. There she observed and documented the remarkable clinical improvements in patients with circulatory and degenerative diseases in response to healthful lifestyle changes.

Dr. Ludington spent seven years as medical advisor for the *Westbrook Hospital* television series. She is presently a health columnist for several publications, associate editor of *Lifeline Health Letter* and medical director of the Lifestyle Medicine Institute in Loma Linda. Dr. Ludington is a popular radio and seminar speaker, particularly in the area of weight control. She recently completed her third book.

Dedicated...

To the more than 40,000 CHIP graduates who continue to validate these health principles in their daily lives. *Dynamic Health* is used as one of the textbooks in the CHIP (Coronary Health Improvement Project) Program. As a community health transformation model, the CHIP program is designed to empower individuals, couples, families, schools, businesses, governments and social and religious institutions to reduce, arrest and reverse Western killer diseases. These diseases are largely related to our lifestyle patterns and account, according to the surgeon general, for more than 75 percent of the deaths in North America.

To NEWSTART Lifestyle Center and other such live-in programs that demonstrate, month by month, with real people, that the principles presented in this book really work.

Contents

---

*The first letter of these words together form the acronym NEWSTART. See page 240–241.

Preface

In today's world, people can do more for their own health than any doctor, hospital or technological advance. The scientific data confirms that the choices we make hour by hour, day by day, largely determine the state of our health, the diseases we get and, often, even when we will die. The challenge is to educate, motivate and inspire people to replace health-destructive habits with health-enhancing lifestyles.

The profusion of health information flowing through the media is overwhelming, confusing and often contradictory. Today's breakthroughs often become tomorrow's big busts. People long for common-sense information that is reliable, understandable and scientifically sound.

Dynamic Health speaks to that need. In this book, a broad range of health information has been broken down into fifty-two brief, concise chapters. Study one chapter each week, and do its corresponding "assignment." Or, read through the entire book and select helpful changes you can make to your lifestyle gradually. At the end of a year you will not only look better and feel younger, but you will also have a sound, basic knowledge of nutritional principles, the causes and treatments of today's common diseases, and a clear understanding of how to manage your own life for maximum health and well-being.

SECTION ONE

HEALTH OUTLOOK

Balance

Costs

Western Diet

Nutrition

Children

Aging

Too Many
Carrots

I t was headline news: Carrots may prevent head and neck cancer. New research suggests that eating five or six of the crunchy tubers a day appears to reverse leukoplakia—a precancerous lesion occurring in the mouth and throat.

My friend Judith promptly purchased a machine that turned fresh carrots into juice.

"How much juice do you get from five carrots?" I asked her one day.

Her eyes flashed. "Oh, I don't stop there. With this machine I can drink five or six pounds of carrots every day!"

Was that a good idea?

It's true that vegetables are an important part of a healthful diet. It's also true that they are increasingly being valued for their role in preventing disease.

But five pounds of one vegetable every day?

Judith's body eventually rebelled. Her skin took on a sickly yellowish color. Fearing hepatitis, she rushed to the doctor. He explained that carrots contain an orange-yellow dye known as beta carotene. The body handles reasonable quantities of this substance, but excessive amounts are stashed away in the liver, skin and mucous membranes, turning them the color of a carrot.

Did that experience straighten her out?

For the moment. But we humans are a curious lot. Sensationalized discoveries and quick solutions to complex health problems are almost irresistible. Before the carrot caper, Judith was swept into the excitement over oat bran. After months of mush and muffins, however, her excitement subsided, and she was ready for a change.

Do carrots actually protect us from cancer?

Carrots and other yellow fruits and vegetables are rich in beta carotene, the substance that began to change Judith's skin color. Beta carotene, which the body turns into vitamin A, is also a substance that appears to protect the body against certain cancers.

Vitamins can be divided into two basic types—those that are water-soluble (dissolve in water) and those that are fat-soluble (dissolve in fat). Water-soluble vitamins (B-complex and C) are not a special concern, because excess amounts can usually be washed out through the kidneys.

But fat-soluble vitamins (A, D, E and K) are another story. Any excess cannot be eliminated except as it is used. In excessive amounts, vitamin A begins to act like a toxin (poison) and may cause headaches, joint pains, damaged skin and hair loss. Because of this potential for toxicity, laws now limit the amount of vitamin A and other fat-soluble vitamins that can be put into supplements.

Beta carotene apparently doesn't have such limits. When the body receives beta carotene, it can make as much vitamin A as it needs and use the rest in other ways. That is one reason the trend these days is to substitute beta carotene for vitamin A in vitamin capsules and tablets.

This distinction is important because it illustrates how the body uses food. Vitamins, minerals and other nutrients in whole foods occur naturally in exactly the right forms for the body to use; it can pick and choose what it needs. But when we consume one food or nutrient in excess, or tamper with the makeup of food, the whole balance can be upset.

So beta carotene is good, but a whole lot of it isn't necessarily better.

Balance is a hard message for today's world. People do nearly everything to excess—they eat too much, drink too much, smoke too much, spend too much and party too much. *Moderation* is about as popular a concept as *wholesomeness*. Then too, we live in an instant society with a quick-fix mentality. It is difficult to accept that instant good health is not automatic as well. Each time a new fad splashes through the media, there is no shortage of takers.

When I was a consultant for a popular health publication, I received a lot of phone calls from reporters who would try to get me to endorse their *fads*. They wanted me to say things like: "Yes, eating a pound of alfalfa sprouts every day will strengthen the heart," or "Several capsules of rooted seaweed will ensure a good night's sleep." No one asked to hear my message about the *balanced diet* that the body needs. I soon realized that a healthful, balanced lifestyle didn't grab headlines, sell magazines (even health magazines) or create profitable new markets for food products.

The human body is able to tolerate excesses of one kind or another for a long time—even six pounds of carrots a day! But the bottom line is that *balance*, not only in what we eat, but also in our total lifestyle, is the key to enduring health and happiness.

Chapter Summary

Too much of a good thing is a bad thing when your health is involved. Common sense and moderation will do more for you than any health fad or miracle cure. Balance is the key to good health—learn to apply it in all areas of your life.

Now that you have examined the principle of balance, take a moment to examine how it applies to your life. Is there an area in your life that is out of balance? If so, write it here:

_____

_____

What are some things you could do this week to bring more balance to this part of your life? List your ideas:

_____

_____

AN ASSIGNMENT

Understanding that balance is the key to a healthful, happy life, make a commitment to act on the ways you have written that will bring more balance into your life. Choose simple ways to make the principle of balance work for you.

The Dollars and Sense of Wellness

A s healthcare costs in America continue to rise at an unprecedented rate, more and more companies are realizing that ailing employees lead to ailing profits.

Is that why healthcare insurance is getting so expensive?

Consider this: Cardiovascular disease costs this nation $274 billion each year, including expenditures and lost productivity. About 58 million Americans (almost one-fourth of the population) live with some form of this disease. That amounts to $4,724 per person per year for each of the 58 million "patients."

That's scary. What is happening? What can people do?

Outside of on-the-job hazards, the biggest threat to an employee's health can be his own lifestyle. Studies have convincingly demonstrated that a rich diet, sedentary living, drinking and smoking, excess weight and elevated blood pressure largely determine a person's risk for developing today's killer diseases. These diseases include heart disease, stroke, adult diabetes, liver cirrhosis and cancers of the lungs, breast, prostate and colon.

A startling report comes from a study comparing average annual employee medical claim costs to the number of risk factors present in each claimant. Risk factors for disease affect medical costs as follows:

- Zero risk factors $250
- One risk factor $450
- Two to three risk factors $750
- Four to five risk factors $1,200
- Six or more risk factors $3,100

These figures clearly demonstrate that these diseases, which are responsible for so much premature death and disability, are directly related to lifestyle factors, which people can control.

Can you explain how lifestyle changes can actually cut healthcare costs?

Here are a few examples:

- Coca Cola reported a reduction in healthcare claims with an exercise program alone, saving $500 per employee per year for the employees (60 percent) who joined their Health Works fitness program.

- Prudential Insurance Company reports the company's major medical costs dropped from $574 to $312 for each participant in its wellness program.

- Smoking kills an average of 1,200 Americans a day and costs $1 billion a week in extra healthcare and insurance costs.

- Pacific Bell's Fit Works participants claim $300 less per case for a one-year savings of $700,000 for the company.

How do companies motivate their employees to do what is good for them?

Many creative ideas are being tried as companies become more serious about reducing health costs. Here are a few examples:

- Many larger companies are installing in-house gymnasiums.

- Some companies have offered monetary awards per overweight pound lost and kept off for a six-month period.

- Other companies are offering generous bonuses to those who quit smoking and to employees who adopt and follow a regular exercise program.

- Another motivator is a big year-end bonus to workers who miss less than four workdays during the year.

The stereotypical businessman—overweight, exhausted, living on cigarettes and three-martini lunches—is out-of-date. In today's business world, *sweat* is status and *trimness* is success. More and more modern executives are apt to be in prime condition; neither they nor their companies can afford otherwise.

The message is clear: People are a company's most valuable asset, and they are worth the investment it takes to keep them healthy. Healthy workers accomplish more, and they cost the company less. Anything a company can do to encourage the health of its workers makes sound *dollar$* and good *$en$e.*

What are the benefits?

Getting healthy can save you money, but of course, the best benefits of health are not financial. They are the benefits you can enjoy every day in the form of increased energy, freedom from disease and a longer, happier life.

Chapter Summary

The poor health of employees costs business and government billions of dollars each year. Many companies are now encouraging their employees to adopt healthier lifestyles because a healthy workforce helps keep costs down and profits up.

An Assignment

Instead of snacking on salty, high-fat chips, try this money-saving alternative:

Crisped Tortilla Chips

1 pkg. of 12 corn tortillas
½ tsp. onion powder
½ tsp. garlic powder

Arrange the tortillas in a stack. Cut the stack into quarters and then cut each quarter in half. Lay the wedges on nonstick baking sheets. Avoid overlapping the pieces. Sprinkle them with onion and garlic powder (optional). Bake in a preheated, 375–400° oven until the chips are crisp.

From Kernel to Colonel

Forty percent of America's food dollars are spent *eating out.* Our food is processed, refined, concentrated, sugared, salted and chemically engineered to produce high-calorie, low-nutrient taste sensations. Our cattle are fattened in feedlots without exercise and with antibiotics and growth enhancers. The result: bigger cattle producing juicier steaks containing nearly twice the fat as range-fed cattle. And we are paying dearly for these *advancements*. While we eat to live, what we eat is killing us.

Are you saying food can cause disease?

The statistics are pretty convincing. One hundred years ago, around 10–15 percent of Americans died from coronary heart disease and strokes. Today it's around 40 percent. Back then, less than 6 percent died of cancer, while today the figure is approaching 26 percent.

This isn't *nature's way.* We weren't meant to die in such numbers from heart attacks, strokes, diabetes, and colon and breast cancer. Significant cardiovascular disease began to emerge in America after World War I. It became really rampant after World War II when people could afford diets rich in animal products and when the food industry began producing highly processed foods crammed with calories and emptied of nutrition.

Could this be coincidental?

Hardly. This problem is unique to Westernized peoples. Rural populations in China, Japan and Southeast Asia who had little access to rich and processed foods experienced few heart attacks. Similarly, most people in rural Africa and South and Central America had little fear of diabetes and cardiovascular disease. Yet in North America, Australia, New Zealand and the increasingly affluent countries in Europe and Asia, where diets are rich in fat, heart disease, cancer, diabetes, obesity and hypertension are epidemic.

The villains, low fiber and high fat, take their toll by damaging the body's vital oxygen-carrying arteries and by upsetting important metabolic functions. Because of thickened, narrowed arteries, *four thousand Americans have heart attacks every day, every third adult has high blood pressure,* and thousands are crippled from strokes. Because of disordered metabolisms from unbalanced lifestyles, obesity is epidemic, and *a new diabetic is diagnosed every 50 seconds.*

How did these dietary changes come about?

Before the twentieth century, the American diet consisted mostly of foods grown in local gardens and nearby farms, supplemented with a few staples from the general store and meat from barnyard animals and range-fed cattle. Our grandparents didn't have thousands of beautifully packaged and highly promoted food products waiting at the supermarket. Fast-food restaurants didn't beckon from nearly every street corner.

The backbone of the diet was kernels—kernels of wheat and other grains growing in reassuring profusion. Families ate freshly cooked food and thick slices of home-baked bread around their own tables. They enjoyed hot cereals, cornbread and biscuits. They ate rice, pasta and corn, along with beans, potatoes, vegetables and fruit. These nutritious high-fiber foods made up the larger percentage of their total daily calorie intake.

But times and tastes have changed dramatically. Freshly cooked breakfast cereals have largely been replaced by cold, presweetened flakes. Lunch typically consists of a salad soaked in oily dressing, or a hamburger, fries and a soda, or perhaps pizza. Dinner often comes frozen in a cardboard box or from the Colonel. Between meals there are sodas, chips and doughnuts. Nutritious, high-fiber foods now represent only 22 percent of our daily calories, while fat consumption has nearly doubled and sugar intake has increased 240 percent.

That's frightening! What can be done?

Education is the key. As people learn that refining food robs it of most of its fiber and nutrients and that processing food adds calories, subtracts nutrition and contributes scores of chemical additives, many are willing to make changes.

People are also realizing that meat and dairy products should be used sparingly. While they do contain nutrients, most are high in fat, cholesterol and calories, and they contain virtually no fiber.

Today's people are increasingly giving up their preoccupation with rich animal products and processed foods and eating more complex carbohydrates—whole plant foods, which are rich in fiber. In 1970 the consumption of meat, whole milk and eggs began to decrease, and so did the number of heart attacks and strokes. But that's changing again. Over the last ten years, cheese, meat, sugar and salt are clearly on the upswing. And so are the Western killer diseases.

The choice is yours. You can have the same freedom from heart disease, stroke and cancer that our ancestors enjoyed simply by changing your habits of diet and exercise. It's possible. All you need are the three essential keys:

The Three Essentials

1. **Desire.** To modify a habit you must want to change. Old patterns are comfortable. To break their grip you need a strong desire to energize you.

2. **Knowledge.** Desire alone cannot change entrenched lifestyle patterns. You must also know *what* to change and understand *why* you should change it.

   For example, although everyone wants to avoid heart disease, achieving this is impossible without the knowledge of the harmful effects of excess cholesterol and fat in the diet.

3. **Skills.** Just knowing what to do to maintain health is not enough.

You need to know *how* to do it and then practice until the new behavior becomes automatic.

Skills that promote health include learning how to cook low-fat meals, developing a program of regular exercise, reading food labels to avoid highly salted products and becoming skilled at choosing healthful food at restaurants.

CHAPTER SUMMARY

Some one hundred years ago, only a fraction of Americans suffered from heart disease, stroke and cancer compared to the number of Americans today with these diseases. Currently, lifestyle-related illnesses account for the majority of deaths in North America. The good news is that you don't have to become a disease-related statistic. By adopting better diet and lifestyle habits, you can live longer and enjoy a healthier, more productive life.

AN ASSIGNMENT

To demonstrate how *the three essentials* can be applied in your life, try a simple experiment. Eat one or two fresh fruit every morning for the next three weeks.

Seven Wrong Roads

As Americans, we pride ourselves on being the best-fed nation on earth. But we are paying a high price for the privilege—in needless disease, disability and premature death.

What are we doing wrong?

Americans are eating too much of nearly everything—too much sugar, too much fat and too much salt. We eat too many calories and too much cholesterol. And we eat too often.

Such *abundance* has helped lay the foundation for coronary artery disease, stroke, high blood pressure, arthritis, adult-onset diabetes, obesity and several kinds of cancer. These diseases are responsible for three out of four deaths. They are related to lifestyle, especially to how we eat.

Disease from eating? You must mean from pesticides and preservatives!

Surprisingly, pesticides and preservatives aren't the worst offenders. Here are some of the more serious culprits:

- *Sugar.* The National Research Council reports that refined sugars and sweeteners account for up to 20 percent of many people's daily calories. Devoid of fiber and nutrients, refined sugars are *empty,* or *naked,* calories. And because of their caloric density, they are well suited to promote obesity.

- *Refined foods.* People used to think refining food was good because it got rid of *useless roughage.* Now we are learning how necessary fiber is in protecting us from certain cancers, stabilizing blood sugar, controlling weight and preventing gastrointestinal problems such as gallstones, hemorrhoids, diverticulitis and constipation.

- *Salt.* Most people in Western cultures consume between 10 and 20 grams of salt a day. (That's 2–4 teaspoons.) This is many times more than the 1 gram ($\frac{1}{5}$ teaspoon) that is needed. This overconsumption of salt contributes prominently to high blood pressure, heart failure and kidney disease.

- *Fat.* Most people don't realize that they are consuming about 36–40 percent of their daily calories as fat. This is much more than the body can properly handle. As a result, blood vessels plug up, impotence sets in, and heart and brain suffer. A high-fat diet also contributes to being overweight, adult diabetes and certain cancers.

- *Proteins.* A diet heavy in meat and animal products provides more protein, fat and cholesterol than the body can use. Americans and other Western cultures eat two to three times more protein than is recommended. Scientists now recognize that a diet containing less protein and much less fat and cholesterol is essential for improved health and longevity.

- *Beverages.* Most North Americans don't drink enough water. Instead, they average several servings of soda, beer, coffee, tea and other sweet drinks every day. Because most of these drinks are loaded with calories, yet lack fiber, they can play havoc with blood sugar levels and sabotage weight control efforts. Alcohol, caffeine, phosphates and other chemicals found in these beverages pose additional health risks.

- *Snacks.* Engineered taste sensations are taking the place of real food. Schools, day-care centers, even hospitals require snacks to be available. The coffee break remains standard in work places, along with after-school and TV snacks at home. Well-planned family meals are now the exception. Snack attacks disrupt digestion, overburden the stomach and are a frequent cause of bloating and indigestion.

So we're eating too much fat.

As you've noticed, fat is one of the prime offenders in the Western diet. We eat too much of it. About 40 percent of the calories in the typical diet come from fat. Research, however, suggests this total should be under 20 percent.

Americans have a "fat tooth," and they pay for it with heart attacks, strokes, obesity and other diseases.

What about salads? There's no fat there.

One of the best places to cut the fat is on your salad. Too many people take nutritious greens and turn them into a high-fat nightmare by adding thick, oily dressings. Restaurants are notorious for this. At most of them you don't get a little dressing to go with your salad—you get a little salad to go with your dressing.

Next time your waiter hands you a menu, order your salad with a low-calorie dressing on the side. Better yet, ask for lemon wedges and squeeze the juice on yourself. It's a tasty, low-calorie, no-fat alternative.

Is there anything SAFE to eat?

Think fruit—hundreds of varieties, spectacular colors and every imaginable texture and flavor. Also, consider endless varieties of vegetables and tubers. In the legume family one finds scores of shapes, colors and flavors. The whole grains present another gold mine of delectable and healthful foods.

People need to realize that eating a variety of whole-plant foods will furnish all the fat, protein, fiber and nutrients the body needs. It is also ecologically sensitive and will cut the food budget in half.

CHAPTER SUMMARY

Too much and too many! Too much sugar, salt, fat, cholesterol and protein create health problems. Too many refined foods, beverages and snacks in our diet are a deadly mix. Only by eating less of these substances and eating more whole-plant foods can we enjoy optimum health and energy.

An Assignment

Four tablespoons of blue cheese or ranch dressing add 300 calories to a salad. That is 300 calories you don't need. This week try your salads with lemon, or mix up some super salad dressing using this recipe.

Super Salad Dressing

¼ cup water
¼ cup lemon juice
¼ tsp. garlic powder
¼ tsp. Italian seasoning
¼ tsp. onion salt

Combine all ingredients and shake well. It gets better with age.

Getting
Fatter

More American children are getting fatter faster than ever. Four to six million youngsters aged six to eleven have serious weight problems, and the number of super-fat children has doubled during the last fifteen years.

That's hard to believe. Isn't our culture more health conscious now? Aren't fitness clubs booming?

Physical fitness is a trend among adults, not children. Grownups are out running, walking, jogging and joining fitness clubs and aerobic classes. Adults flock to wellness lectures and examine menus at restaurants for healthier and leaner foods. Meanwhile, the media entice our children with highly refined, caloric "goodies."

But don't schools have health courses, physical education and sports activities?

Due to budget cuts, overcrowding and teacher shortages, many schools have had to cut back on these programs in recent years. In some cases they have eliminated physical education courses and requirements altogether. Health classes are often unpopular with students, and relatively few youngsters qualify for team positions in school-sponsored sports.

Isn't obesity in children mostly inherited?

Genes do play a role in a person's weight, but they aren't the whole answer. Environment plays a critically important role—as shown by the fact that the percentage of obese Americans has increased steadily over the past fifty years. Our gene pool can't change that fast!

There was a time when children raced home from school to change clothes and go outside to play. They climbed trees, rode bicycles, skated, played games and dribbled basketballs. Today's children average five to eight hours a day watching television or playing computer games!

What are the chances of a fat child becoming a fat adult?

About 80 percent of overweight teenagers will remain overweight as adults. The increase in adolescent obesity (about 40 percent during the last fifteen years) will have serious consequences in the future.

Does obesity produce disease in childhood?

Being overweight predisposes a child to heart disease, gallstones, adult-onset diabetes, hypertension, cancer and full-blown obesity later in life. Obese children have more orthopedic problems and upper respiratory diseases. And that is only one side of the story. They often suffer major social and psychological problems. The rapid increase of serious depression, eating disorders, drug use and suicide among teenagers is frightening.

What can be done about this growing problem?

The major causes of obesity in children are the same as for adults— a sedentary lifestyle, TV viewing, computers, the snack and soda habit, and the popularity and availability of highly processed and concentrated foods. Many major medical centers are developing weight control programs for children that involve the whole family. Proper eating and lifestyle habits are a family affair, and a youngster especially needs the support of the family. Even when the rest of the family is not overweight, everyone benefits from a healthier way of life.

Nearly all obesity in children could be prevented if they were taught the following sensible basic habits early, before they have free access to food and become addicted to TV and computer games:

- Three meals a day with lots of whole grains, legumes, fresh fruit and vegetables.

- No snacks or sodas between meals.

- Drink plenty of water.

- An hour or two of active exercise daily, preferably outdoors.

- Regular, quiet study and reading times to replace the hours spent watching TV and sitting at the computer.

- Plenty of rest. Many children are chronically tired. Put them to bed early enough so they awaken naturally, in time for a healthy breakfast.

- A wide range of interests—library visits, music lessons, arts and crafts, family outings and so forth.

The Bible says:

> Train a child in the way he should go, and when he is old he will not turn from it.
> —PROVERBS 22:6, NIV

Saving the child just might save the family.

CHAPTER SUMMARY

Hours of television, Nintendo and the easy availability of high-calorie snacks are creating a generation of super-fat children. Their obesity predisposes them to a host of lifestyle-related illnesses and has been linked to serious psychological problems. Families can help these children by adopting proper eating and lifestyle habits. Good health is a family affair.

AN ASSIGNMENT

Use the ideas you came up with in this unit to make your home a place where good eating habits can flourish. Involve your family in the changes.

Older Can
Be Better

Everyone hates getting old. People want to stay young or at least middle-aged. But time keeps marching. With the *sixty-five and older* segment getting larger in North America, what are the prospects for the golden-agers in today's world?

An increasing trend is to date people by their intellectual and social capabilities rather than by chronological age. Health, rather than years, usually determines one's status.

Old age sets in when disease and disability limit everyday tasks. Some people are old while still relatively young in years. These are usually people who are chronically ill, injured or victims of a major tragedy, many of whom withdraw and give up on life. Others remain youthful, vital, interesting and productive into advanced age.

Some people claim older is better. Can that be?

It's a matter of perspective. For physical strength, energy and fewer ailments, youth is better. But for increased confidence, better judgment and insight, less anxiety and more freedom, older can be better. And experience helps, too. Most philosophers, composers, painters and writers, for instance, improve with time and life experiences.

Don't most people over sixty-five suffer from chronic illnesses?

In affluent Western society, about 80 percent of the sixty-five-and-over group have some kind of health problem such as high blood pressure, arthritis or heart disease. But most illnesses are not incapacitating. About 95 percent of older people live in their communities, and most have their own households.

Premature aging and disability are largely the result of lifestyle factors such as smoking, excessive alcohol and caffeine consumption, and the abuse of drugs. Being overweight speeds up physical and sexual decline. A diet of rich, refined foods and lack of regular exercise can make people old before their time.

Isn't forgetfulness a bad sign?

Forgetfulness in older people is exaggerated. Stress, anxiety, fast-moving events, memory overload and lack of interest can cause forgetfulness at any age. Depression, which affects many older people, is often misdiagnosed as senility. Only a few people develop Alzheimer's disease or other genuinely senile dementia. Most people retain remarkable memory function for a long time, especially when they stay active and fit.

Don't many older people end up in nursing homes?

Actually, in North America only 2 percent of people sixty-four to seventy-five years of age live in nursing homes. Only after age eighty-five does the figure reach 20 percent.

Today is a good time to be alive! Productive social activities are pushing back the aging process. So are exercise, a better understanding of the role of diet, earlier attention to health problems and advances in modern technology. People today are often staying physically and mentally fit into their eighties and nineties. Many remain sexually active as well.

There is more. Scientists are discovering that an optimistic, positive attitude actually boosts the body's immune mechanism. This sophisticated defense system is proving to be one of the major keys to good health. The Good Book said it long ago: "A merry heart does good, like medicine" (Prov. 17:22, NKJV).

Aren't there active seniors?

At age sixty-six, Hulda Crooks decided to take on a new challenge— mountain climbing. In the twenty-five years since, she has scaled some of North America's tallest peaks. Recently, she became the oldest woman ever to ascend Mt. Fuji, the tallest mountain in Japan.

Mrs. Crooks is not alone. Newspaper articles recently chronicled the success of an eighty-year-old Seattle man. He climbed 14,000 feet to stand on the pinnacle of ice-covered Mt. Rainier.

Not everyone wants to test their endurance on the world's great mountains, but we all want to live productive, useful lives. As you are discovering, a healthful diet and sound lifestyle practices can keep you going strong in your later years. How you treat your body today will influence your health tomorrow and far into the future.

What can I do now to plan for my future?

Take a moment to imagine yourself on your ninetieth birthday. Are you standing atop a mountain? Painting a picture? Celebrating life with family and friends? Or are you ill and isolated?

Research confirms that a positive attitude is important for physical health and happiness. Without purpose, goals and productive social activities, we age quickly. Do you have interests and goals that will carry you through your lifetime?

In the space below, list three interests or goals you would like to pursue. Is there something you have always wanted to try? Some place you want to visit? Something you hope to contribute? Use your imagination and list them on the lines below.

_____

_____

CHAPTER SUMMARY

A diet of rich, refined foods and a lack of exercise can make you old before your time. But with a healthy lifestyle, worthwhile goals and a positive mental attitude, it is possible to enjoy life well into your golden years.

AN ASSIGNMENT

They say you are as young as you feel. Start feeling younger by taking that first small step toward a meaningful goal. Learning to create your own purpose and goals (rather than relying on work or family responsibilities to create them for you) is one way to ensure healthy and happy senior years.

LIFESTYLE DISEASES

Coronary Heart Disease

Reversing Heart Disease

Hypertension

Stroke

Cancer

Diabetes

Osteoporosis

Obesity

Killer for Dinner

Hundreds of thousands of people died last year from heart attacks without a murmur of protest from the public, the press or government agencies. Yet the nation's number one killer can be found right on the dinner table!

You mean, what we eat causes heart attacks?

Not everything. The main culprits are excessive amounts of fat and cholesterol. The underlying problem is a hardening, a plugging up of vital arteries that supply the heart with oxygenated blood, a process known as *atherosclerosis*.

People are born with clean, flexible arteries, which should stay that way throughout life. The arteries of many North Americans, however, are clogging up with cholesterol, fat and calcium—a concoction that gradually hardens and eventually chokes off needed oxygen supplies.

During World War II most Europeans were forced to change their eating habits from their customary diet of meat, eggs and dairy products to a more austere diet of potatoes, grains, beans, roots and vegetables. The result? A dramatic decrease in atherosclerosis, which lasted for several years.

Since then, massive amounts of data have accumulated from research on animals and humans around the world. The results are essentially the same: Diets high in fat and cholesterol produce elevated levels of blood cholesterol and heart disease. Diets low in fat and cholesterol reduce blood cholesterol levels and the risk of heart disease, and they can reverse the atherosclerotic plaque buildup.

How can I tell if I have atherosclerosis?

There simply aren't any hints of the problem until your arteries are seriously narrowed. Some people begin to experience angina (heart pain) on exertion. For many people a heart attack is the first sign of trouble. About one-third of heart attacks result in sudden death.

Who is at risk for heart attack?

Risk Factors in Heart Disease

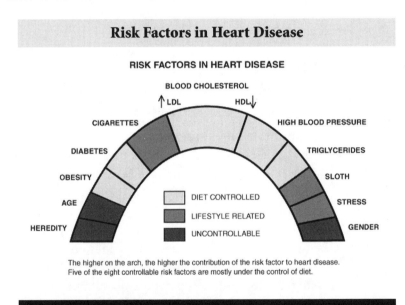

RISK FACTORS IN HEART DISEASE

The higher on the arch, the higher the contribution of the risk factor to heart disease.
Five of the eight controllable risk factors are mostly under the control of diet.

The risk factor concept is a good way to determine the likelihood of coronary heart disease:

- The most serious risk factor by far is an elevated blood cholesterol. Fifty-year-old men with cholesterol levels over 295 mg/dl (or 7.6 mmol/L) are nine times more likely to develop atherosclerosis than men the same age with levels under 200 mg/dl (or 5.1 mmol/L). A 20 percent decrease in a person's blood cholesterol level lowers his risk of a coronary by 40–50 percent.

- By age sixty, smokers are ten times more likely to die from heart disease than nonsmokers. Over 160,000 coronary deaths a year are related to smoking, about 30 percent of the total.

- In North America every third adult has high blood pressure and is three times more likely to die of heart disease than a person with normal blood pressure.

- Obese men are five times more likely to die of heart disease by age sixty than men of normal weight.

- Other risk factors are diabetes, elevated triglycerides, sedentary lifestyle and stress.

All of the above risk factors can be controlled by changes in diet and lifestyle. Heredity, age and gender are risk factors a person cannot control, but they are fortunately the least important.

What about medications and surgery?

For those with dangerous cholesterol levels that do not respond adequately to diet, medications may be needed. Medications, however, are expensive, and most have serious side effects. They require frequent laboratory tests and physician checkups.

More glamorous are the surgical procedures: bypass operations, roto-rooter cleanouts and balloon stretching. Some results have been spectacular. But as time goes on and statistics accumulate, it is becoming apparent that most of these operations do not prolong life or even necessarily improve it. Medical treatment is temporary at best. The only long-term solution is a serious lifestyle change.

So what is the best approach?

The best possible approach is prevention, and it is never too late to start. Even if heart disease has developed, as suggested by the presence of coronary risk factors and documented by diagnostic tests, it still isn't too late to make lifestyle changes. You can actually clean out your arteries, lower your risk of dying of atherosclerosis and extend your active, productive years. You can markedly change your risk factors no matter how old you are, often in just a few weeks.

Start with healthful, home-cooked meals that are very low in fat and cholesterol, yet high in unrefined complex carbohydrates and fiber. Such a diet can lower cholesterol levels by 20–30 percent and normalize most cases of adult diabetes in less than four weeks. When combined with salt restriction, this diet will also help normalize blood pressure and control obesity.

And begin an active, daily exercise program.

If Americans would lower their cholesterol to below 180, their blood pressures to under 125 and quit smoking, it has been estimated that 82 percent of all heart attacks before age sixty-five could be prevented. These simple changes in lifestyle would do more to improve the health of our nation than all the hospitals, surgeries and drugs put together.

How can I identify my risk factor for heart disease?

The *HeartScreen* test on pages 30–31 will help you identify and understand your own risk factors and guide you in dealing with them. It will approximate your relative risk and will help you identify areas that you may want to work on. In this test, eight risk factors are listed, and scores from 1 to 8 are assigned to each factor.

CHAPTER SUMMARY

We are born with clean, flexible arteries, but excessive fat and cholesterol in the diet can clog them. Eventually this chokes off the oxygen supply to vital organs. Most medical treatment is temporary, at best. If we want to stop heart disease from being the number one killer in North America, lifestyle change is the most promising solution.

AN ASSIGNMENT

If you don't know your cholesterol, triglycerides and blood pressure levels, you need to find out. See your physician. The test takes only a few minutes. Make an appointment this week. What you learn as a result of this test can help save your life.

HeartScreen

Self-Scoring Test of Heart Attack and Stroke Risk

Risk Level and Score

Risk Factor	0	1	2	3	4	5	6	7	8
1. Cholesterol* (mg%)	under 160	160–179	180–199	200–219	220–239	240–259	260–279	280–299	over 300
2. Blood pressure* (mmHg)	under 110	110–119	120–129	130–139	140–159	over 160			
3. Smoking (cig./day)	none	up to 5	5–9	10–19	20–29	over 30			
4. Overweight** (in %)	0–4%	5–9%	10–14%	15–19%	20–29%	over 30%			
5. Triglycerides* (mg%)	under 100	100–149	150–249	250–349	over 350				
6. Diabetes (duration)	none	under 5 years	5–10 years	over 10 years					
7. Resting pulse beats/min.	under 56	56–62	63–69	70–80	over 80				
8. Stress	rarely tense	tense 3x/wk	tense 2–3x/day	tense & rushed	on tranquilizers				

Risk Factor	Score
Cholesterol	
Blood pressure	
Smoking	
Overweight	
Triglycerides	
Diabetes	
Pulse	
Stress	
Total Score:	

* To determine your cholesterol, triglycerides, and blood pressure, just see your physician. The blood test is very simple, inexpensive, takes about five minutes, and it will tell you a lot!

** To determine your percentage of overweight, look up your ideal weight (see chapter 21) and subtract it from your actual weight. Divide the difference in pounds by your ideal weight and multiply by 100.

HeartScreen: Interpreting Your Score

0–6 **Ideal**	Development of heart disease or stroke is extremely unlikely, especially if your cholesterol level is below 160.
7–14 **Elevated**	The development of heart disease or stroke is about one-third of the U.S. average, yet three times higher than for the Ideal group.
15–22 **High**	This is the average. You cannot afford to be average because your risk is ten times higher than the Ideal group.
23–30 **Very High Risk**	The development of heart disease and stroke is about three times the U.S. average, or 30 times higher than the Ideal group. Action is imperative! You may be able to drop four to six points within four to eight weeks by lowering cholesterol and blood pressure through dietary change.
31–38 **Danger**	The likelihood of having a heart attack or stroke is about four to six times the U.S. average and about fifty times higher than the Ideal group. Set goals and take action without delay!

Eat Your Way Out

The sports world rejoiced when former Yale president Dr. Bart Giamotti became commissioner of baseball. A few months later a shocked nation wept when this respected man died suddenly at age fifty-one from a heart attack.

Scenarios like this one are repeated thousands of times each day across North America. Heart disease now strikes a deadly blow to four out of every ten Americans.

Is there a solution? Does it have to be like this?

Yes…and no.

As long as Americans continue to eat their rich, fatty diet, these statistics will continue to worsen. We have known for years that a high-fat, high-cholesterol diet is the primary cause of coronary heart disease.

But there is a solution: It requires that we *lean out* our high-fat diet. To the extent that we do this, we can help prevent and even reverse heart disease.

Are you saying that heart disease may be curable?

It looks very promising that you can cure your heart disease, according to the accumulating results of medical studies.

The idea took on a life of its own when Dean Ornish, MD, published a report in the *Lancet* medical journal, in 1990, that shook up the medical community. Dr. Ornish spent one year studying fifty men with advanced heart disease, many of whom were candidates for coronary bypass surgery.

He randomly assigned the men to different groups. Both groups were asked to quit smoking and to walk daily. In addition, the first group practiced stress management and followed a vegetarian diet with less than 10 percent of calories as fat and no cholesterol.

The second group was given the American Heart Association's "Prudent Diet" for heart disease. This diet allowed 30 percent of calories as fat and up to 300 mg of cholesterol a day.

At the end of the year, when the results were presented at the scientific session of the American Heart Association in Washington, D.C., they became front-page news all over America.

Dr. Ornish reported that those on the very low-fat vegetarian diet not only dropped their dangerous LDL-cholesterol level average by 37 percent, but also their narrow, plaque-filled arteries had actually widened, allowing more blood and oxygen to the heart muscle. The heart disease had, in fact, begun to reverse itself. And the older men with the more advanced disease actually had the best results.

The group on the so-called Prudent Diet, however, had virtually no cholesterol drop, and their coronary arteries showed increased narrowing. Their heart disease had actually gotten worse.

You mean the American Heart Association's diet did not help at all?

It appears that the Prudent Diet designed for the prevention and treatment of heart disease does not do its job. At the press conference Dr. Ornish concluded: "The moderate diet recommendations of the American Heart Association do not go far enough to effectively influence the progression of coronary heart disease. People with clinically demonstrated disease need to go beyond the present dietary recommendation."

We have known for years that much of today's heart disease could be *prevented*, but it is exciting to realize that, under the proper conditions, it is possible to *reverse* it. This revolutionary concept is now being implemented in many centers and cities; given the proper diet, we can now eat ourselves out of heart disease.

Calorie Concentration: How Fats Do It!

Food	Cal.		Empty Calories	Cal.	Total Calories
Lettuce and Tomato Salad	40	+	Roquefort Dressing	160	200
Whole-Wheat Bread (1 slice)	65	+	Butter	70	135
Broccoli (½ cup)	35	+	Cheese Sauce	130	165
Vegetarian Entree or Broiled Fish (6 oz.)	220	+	Tartar Sauce	100	320
Baked Potato with Salsa	135	+	Sour Cream and Butter	180	315
Skim Milk (1 glass)	90	or	Whole Milk		160
Baked Apple with Date or Walnut	100	or	Apple Pie á la Mode (⅙)		480
Total Calories	**685**		**Total Calories**		**1,775**

Heart attacks are the leading cause of death in the United States—and too much fat is the leading cause of heart attacks. It's been said that excess fat is the most harmful element in the Western diet. Isn't it time you reduced the amount you are eating?

Any ideas on lowering fat intake?

Dr. Ornish showed that lowering the fat in the diet can reverse heart disease. But making the switch isn't always easy. Asking an American to switch to a low-fat diet is like asking a Chinese chef to cook Italian food—it certainly can be done, but it takes some effort and the willingness to learn new habits.

Here are four general strategies you can use to reduce the fat in your diet.

> **Substitute:** Drink skim milk instead of whole milk or better yet, use some of the low-fat nondairy substitutes!

Try a bowl of chilled fruit instead of ice cream for dessert. Look for healthful substitutes to the high-fat items in your diet such as cheeses, meats, dressings and oils.

Reduce: Instead of ordering an 8-ounce steak, try a smaller portion with pasta. Instead of a whole piece of pie, take just a sliver. Eating smaller portions of your favorite high-fat foods allows you to savor a few decadent bites while still cutting fat from your diet.

Eliminate: Eliminate as many temptations as possible. If you don't buy it and bring it into the house, you won't eat it when you are tempted!

Construct: Processed foods are stuffed with added fat. If you want to regain control over what goes into your body, cook for yourself. Get a good low-fat cookbook and learn how to prepare delicious new dishes. It's the surest way to protect yourself from the deadly effects of too much fat.

CHAPTER SUMMARY

We have known for years that much of heart disease could be prevented; now we know it can be reversed. Plaque-filled arteries in patients on very low-fat, vegetarian diets actually begin to open up, allowing more blood and oxygen to the heart and other vital organs.

AN ASSIGNMENT

It is your turn to list some specific ways you can apply the principles of *substitution, reduction, elimination* and *construction* to your diet.

Choose at least one of the ways you have listed and put it into practice this week.

The Silent Killer

Every third adult in North America has high blood pressure. These hypertensives are three times more likely to have a heart attack, five times more likely to develop heart failure and eight times more likely to suffer a stroke than are people with normal blood pressure.

How can I know if I have hypertension?

Hypertension is defined as a systolic blood pressure reading (the top number) consistently over 140 and/or a diastolic (lower number) reading of 90 or above. Even though there are no symptoms (that's why it is called the *silent disease*), such conditions cause progressive changes in the blood vessels until the first sign hits, usually a stroke or a heart attack.

What causes the blood pressure to go up?

Certain kinds of tumors will do it, also diseases within the kidney itself. But in 90 percent of everyday hypertension, the specific organic cause cannot be determined. This kind of hypertension is called *essential* hypertension. The following factors contribute to essential hypertension:

- *High salt intake.* Surprisingly, hypertension is uncommon in 70 percent of the world's population. Salt intake is low

36

in these areas. In places where salt intake is high, as in Japan, the disease is epidemic, affecting approximately one-half of adults. Americans consume an average of 10–20 grams of salt per day. As we have mentioned, that is 2–4 teaspoons or about ten to twenty times more than the body needs!

- *Obesity.* Nearly everyone who is significantly overweight will eventually experience high blood pressure. It's just a matter of time.

- *Arterial plaque.* Narrowed and plugged arteries force the body to boost the blood pressure in order to deliver necessary oxygen and food to body cells.

- *Estrogen.* This hormone, found in birth control pills and used to ease menopausal symptoms, is also a salt retainer. It can raise blood pressure by holding excess fluid in the body.

- *Alcohol.* Scientific studies have demonstrated that alcohol intake accounts for 5–15 percent of cases of ordinary hypertension.

What should I do to reduce salt intake?

We all need to reduce the amount of salt we eat. Don't worry about not getting enough. If you are like most Americans, you eat up to twenty times more than you need. Three culprits are responsible for much of this harmful excess.

The salt shaker: Throw it away. You already get a dangerously high amount of salt from the food you eat. Don't add to the problem by pouring more on top. Your food will seem bland for a couple of weeks, but your taste buds will soon adjust, and you will begin to enjoy the subtle flavors of foods. The day will come when foods you now think of as delicious will taste salty.

Salty snacks: Things like potato chips, pretzels and salted nuts are so dangerous they should have a surgeon general's warning on the box that says: "Warning: Salty snacks are linked to hypertension, stroke and heart disease. Eat at your own risk." If you must snack, use substitutes like carrot sticks and sliced apples.

Fast foods: If we would cut our salt intake to 5 grams a day (1 teaspoon), hypertension would virtually disappear. We will never reach that goal, however, until we break the fast-food habit. A McDonald's cheeseburger alone contains 2 grams of salt. And a three-piece chicken dinner from Kentucky Fried Chicken has a whopping 5.6 grams of salt—more than you should eat for an entire day.

Why not just take medications for hypertension?

The past few years have produced an avalanche of new drugs that are effective in lowering blood pressure. Some are lifesaving. Most produce prompt results—the quick fix that Americans love.

But a closer look at hypertension medications reveals some disquieting facts: The drugs do not cure hypertension; they only control it. In many cases the medications need to be taken for life. And many cause unpleasant side effects that include fatigue, depression and lack of sexual desire. While the drugs help protect against strokes, they may not protect against coronary atherosclerosis (the plugging of heart arteries). Some may actually *contribute to* atherosclerosis, diabetes and gouty arthritis.

What are the alternatives?

A number of major scientific studies have shown that *simple* dietary and lifestyle changes can reverse most essential hypertension in a matter of weeks without drugs.

- Most people are probably salt-sensitive and would benefit greatly from its reduction in their diets.

- When the weight goes down, blood pressure levels usually fall. Reducing excess weight is often the only treatment needed to correct a rising blood pressure.

- A low-fat, high-fiber diet lowers the blood pressure about 10 percent even without weight loss or salt restriction. Thinning of the blood, which results from eating less fat, probably produces these favorable changes.

- Deleting alcohol from the diet will lower blood pressure and do the body a favor in several other areas as well.

- Getting more potassium by eating more fruits and vegetables lowers blood pressure.

- Physical exercise lowers blood pressure by reducing peripheral arterial resistance. In addition, regular exercise promotes general health and well-being.

Caution: People taking blood pressure medications should not play doctor and change doses or stop medicines on their own. But those who are willing to make healthful lifestyle changes will usually find their physicians glad to help them eat and exercise their way out of hypertension and to lower their blood pressure medication.

CHAPTER SUMMARY

In North America every third adult has high blood pressure. This puts them at risk of heart attack, stroke and other debilitating diseases. Obesity, narrowed arteries, estrogen, alcohol, low dietary potassium and high salt intake all contribute to the problem. Fortunately, most cases of hypertension can be reversed by simple dietary and lifestyle changes.

AN ASSIGNMENT

A wise general once said, "Know your enemies." Now that you are aware of the three worst culprits (salt shaker, salty snacks, fast foods), it's time to do something about them. What are you willing to do to cut salt intake to a level your body can handle? Put your plan in writing.

Stalking a Crippler

Two million Americans lie crippled from paralyzing strokes. After AIDS and cancer, stroke is probably the most dreaded and disabling disease to afflict Westernized civilizations.

What are a person's chances of developing a stroke?

Every year more than 750,000 Americans have strokes. As with heart attacks, serious and even fatal strokes can occur without warning. Around one-fourth of victims under age seventy die from the first attack; after that the figure doubles.

Of those who survive, 40 percent need some degree of ongoing special care, but only 10 percent require institutionalization.

The remaining 60 percent represent the good news. Some recover completely; nearly all improve enough to care for themselves; most are able to resume their normal activities.

What causes strokes?

A stroke, or cerebral vascular accident (CVA), is most commonly related to atherosclerosis—a thickening, narrowing and hardening of arteries supplying the brain with oxygenated blood. This atherosclerotic process can occur both in arteries within the brain and in arteries leading to the brain. The roughened, ragged inner surfaces of damaged arteries become seedbeds for clot formation and plaque buildup. When obstruction is complete, the artery is said to be *thrombosed.*

Sometimes pieces of plaque or a blood clot break off from other parts of the circulatory system and travel to smaller brain arteries, producing obstruction. These are called *emboli.* Some 85 percent of CVAs result from either thrombotic or embolic arterial blockage.

Hemorrhages, or blowouts, cause the rest of the strokes. Most of these are associated with uncontrolled high blood pressure, which forces blood through cracks in stiffened artery walls. A few blowouts are caused by *aneurysms.* These are ballooned-out areas in certain arteries, where the arterial walls get thinner and thinner until they rupture. The result, either way, is bleeding into the brain.

Who is at risk for strokes?

Most strokes are directly related to high blood pressure. People with hypertension are six times more likely to suffer a stroke than are people with normal blood pressure.

Blackout spells, called *transient ischemic attacks* (TIAs), may be early warnings. These are small strokes, which start suddenly and disappear in less than 24 hours. Most last only a few seconds, and recovery is complete. Persistent TIAs, however, increase the chances for a complete stroke, much as angina attacks increase the chances of a heart attack.

Other risk factors include elevated blood cholesterol and triglycerides, smoking, diabetes, obesity and sedentary lifestyle, all of which contribute to the atherosclerotic process. In fact, the risk factors for stroke are basically the same as those for coronary heart disease, because both diseases are caused by underlying damage to vital, oxygen-carrying arteries.

Can strokes be prevented?

Yes, most strokes can be prevented. In fact, strokes, like certain other lifestyle diseases, could become relatively uncommon within a generation if people would begin adopting, early in life, the healthful lifestyle practices already known today. These include the following:

- Don't smoke. One out of every six CVA deaths is directly related to tobacco use.

- Check blood pressure regularly. Hypertension has no symptoms, and it can sneak up on the unaware. Remember, hypertension increases a person's stroke risk by 800 percent.

- Learn to use much less salt. As we have mentioned, in areas of the world where salt intake is low, hypertension is virtually unknown. In Japan, where salt intake was high, stroke was the leading cause of death.

- Normalize weight. Obesity promotes atherosclerosis, hypertension and most diabetes.

- Eat a low-fat, low-cholesterol, high-fiber diet. Ideally, keeping fat intake to less than 15 percent of daily calories has been shown to protect arterial linings from atherosclerosis.

- Exercise actively and regularly. Exercise improves circulation and helps control weight and hypertension.

What about people who have already had strokes? Is there help for them?

Definitely. The lifestyle that helps prevent strokes will also hasten recovery, as well as help prevent recurrent strokes.

Acute strokes require good nursing care and energetic rehabilitation. In selected cases, surgical procedures such as endarterectomy (cleaning out the arteries) are of value.

Small doses of aspirin have been shown to help prevent certain strokes in susceptible people. Remember, however, that aspirin may also promote bleeding tendencies (including in the brain) and aggravate stomach ulcers.

But the best news is that arterial blockages are reversible. Thickened, narrowed arteries slowly open again when a low-fat vegetarian diet is consistently followed, along with the other health practices. While these studies, so far, center on coronary arteries, similar results are expected in arteries affecting the brain, since the underlying problems are similiar.

Everyone is born with soft, flexible, elastic artery walls. Many populations around the world retain their healthy arteries and low blood pressures throughout their lifetimes. We can, too, if we get serious about pursuing healthful lifestyle practices before the damage is done.

What if I don't use salt?

As we saw in our discussion of hypertension, not salting your food is a good way to start protecting yourself from stroke. Unfortunately, only 25 percent of the salt we eat comes from the shaker. Much of the rest is hidden in processed foods and snacks. Remember, you need only 1 gram, which is about ⅕ of a teaspoon of salt a day. Here are a few examples of quantities of salt you may be eating without knowing it:

Hidden Salt Content

Processed Food	Salt (mg)
Apple pie (1 slice)	1,000
Canned chili with beans (1 cup)	3,000
Minute rice, Long Grain, Wild (1 cup)	1,000
Wheaties (2 ounces)	1,100
Salisbury steak (1 cup)	3,150
Potato chips (7 ounces)	3,500
Tomato sauce (½ cup)	1,950
Canned tomato soup (1 cup)	2,200
Corned beef hash (1 cup)	3,075
Cheese, American (2 slices)	1,950
Kentucky Fried Chicken (3 pieces)	5,775

Become a label reader. When you check the nutrition label on your food, you won't find the word *salt* listed. Instead, you will find the quantity of sodium listed. Since sodium, which is the culprit in salt, makes up 40 percent of the salt by weight, you need to multiply the sodium content by 2.5 to obtain the salt equivalent value.

Don't get tricked. Makers of salty foods often try to hide the fact of high sodium content by providing information based on ridiculously small serving sizes. Don't be fooled—take serving size into account when you buy, as well as when you eat.

CHAPTER SUMMARY

Stroke is one of the most dreaded and disabling diseases afflicting Westernized countries, but it is not a disease that attacks indiscriminately. In many populations around the world, stroke is virtually unknown. You can reduce your risk by adopting a lifestyle that promotes healthy arteries and low blood pressure.

AN ASSIGNMENT

Start checking labels when you shop. Look for low sodium foods or alternatives. And keep the daily salt intake well below 5 grams (5,000 mg), which is the equivalent of 2,000 mg of sodium.

Do-It-Yourself Cancers

M any cancers are turning out to be do-it-yourself diseases. We promote them by chronic exposure to certain environmental factors. What we eat and drink, where we live and work, and what we breathe may well determine whether we become a cancer statistic.

Are you saying that we bring cancer on ourselves?

Medical science continues to make strides toward earlier detection and improved treatments for many cancers. But these efforts are largely *after the fact.* The sad truth is that the overall death rates for many adult cancer patients continue to rise. One in four American lives is now being claimed by cancer.

This trend, however, could be reversed. If we would simply take the precautions that we already know about, 70 percent of the cancers that afflict Americans could be prevented.

Won't people do just about anything to avoid such a terrifying disease?

Almost anything, it seems, except change their lifestyles.

Take lung cancer, for example—the cancer that kills more men and women in the United States than any other. Ever since the surgeon general's report in 1964, we've known that lung cancer is directly related to cigarette smoking. It's true that millions have quit smoking, yet every fourth adult in North America still smokes! Close to 90 percent of lung cancers and 50–80 percent of the cancers of the lip, mouth, tongue, throat and esophagus could be prevented if people simply stopped using tobacco. It would also prevent close to half the bladder cancers.

Are some cancers related to diet?

In men, the second and third most frequently occurring cancers are those of the prostate and colon. For women, the most common after lung cancer are cancers of the breast and colon. Extensive evidence links more than 50 percent of these cancers to "over-nutrition"—too much fat and too much weight.

How about chemicals and pesticides?

Carcinogens (cancer-producing chemicals) are a concern, especially with the array of additives, preservatives, flavor enhancers, pesticides and other chemicals that we use in producing and marketing food. However, only 2 percent of all cancers can be reliably linked to these substances.

In contrast, evidence of the connection between cancer and such dietary factors as fiber and fat grows stronger every day. Compared with diets at the turn of the twentieth century, the average American now eats one-third *more* fat and one-third *less* fiber. In areas of the world where fat intake is low and fiber consumption is high, the prevalence rates of colon, breast and prostate cancers are low. In countries such as the United States, Canada and New Zealand, where diets are low in fiber and high in fat, rates for these kinds of cancers are the highest in the world.

Could racial variations, rather than diet, account for these differences?

Researchers have asked the same question. They have found, for example, that Japanese living in villages and rural areas have very few of these cancers. Their traditional fiber consumption was high, and their fat intake averaged often less than 10 percent of their calories eaten. But when Japanese migrate to America and adopt Western eating habits and lifestyles, their rates for these cancers increase dramatically and soon equal those of Americans.

How can such things as fiber and fat influence cancer?

Not all the answers are in yet, but cancer is associated with carcinogens—chemical irritants that can produce cancerous lesions over time.

Bile acids are an example. The amount of fat in the diet affects the amount of bile the body produces. In the intestinal tract some of these bile acids can form irritating co-carcinogenic compounds. The longer these compounds stay in contact with the lining of the colon, the more irritation results.

This is where fiber comes in. With a low-fiber diet, material moves slowly through the intestines, often taking from seventy-two hours to five days to complete the journey from entry to exit. Fiber absorbs water like a sponge. This helps fill the intestines and stimulates them to increased activity. With a high-fiber diet, food travels through the intestines much faster and completes the journey in twenty-four to thirty-six hours.

This helps the colon in two ways. It shortens the exposure to irritating substances, and it dilutes the concentration of the irritants because of fiber's water-holding ability and insulating effect.

What about other cancers?

A high fat intake depresses the activity of important cells in the body's immune system. This effect has been studied extensively in connection with breast cancer and may well affect other types of cancer as well.

Excessive alcohol consumption increases the risk for cancer of the esophagus and pancreas, and it does so dramatically for those who smoke as well. Excess weight raises the risk of cancer of the breast, colon and prostate. Then there are such things as exposure to asbestos, sidestream smoke and toxic chemicals.

Just four lifestyle factors—no smoking, no alcohol, a high-fiber/low-fat diet rich in fruits and vegetables, grains and legumes, and normal weight—could prevent close to 70 percent of adult cancers found in Western society today. Instead of one American in four dying of cancer, the risk could be reduced to about one in fifteen.

Is this an impossible dream?

No, it's not. Imagine the announcement of a pill that would make people immune to cancer. It would be the news story of the decade. People would flock to their doctors for a prescription, and the inventors would be wealthy beyond belief.

No such pill exists, but we have listed four things that, taken together, can prevent the majority of adult cancers.

How can I move toward an optimal diet?

One of the items on your list should be a very low-fat, low-cholesterol diet. Many studies have shown that such a diet reduces the risk of heart disease, diabetes, stroke and many types of cancer.

One sensible way to move toward an optimal diet is by designating a day or two each week for meals without meat—no steaks, chicken or fish! This gives you a chance to experiment with healthful ways of cooking, while gradually building up a repertoire of favorite new recipes.

Moving Toward the *Optimal Diet*

1. Use whole-grain breads and cereals. They have the vitamins, minerals and fiber that products made with refined flour lack.

2. Enjoy fresh fruit each day. Eat a variety of fresh fruit.

3. Eat a wide variety of vegetables. Dark-green leafy vegetables are essential for good health, and especially for those who chose a strict vegetarian lifestyle. (One cup of certain greens contains more calcium than milk.) Yellow vegetables are high in vitamin A.

4. Use nuts sparingly. They are high in minerals and vitamins but also contain plenty of fat.

5. Use a wide variety of beans and peas. They provide protein and fiber and are low in fat.

CHAPTER SUMMARY

There is a link between lifestyle factors and many cancers. Smoking, obesity, consumption of alcohol and a diet that is high in animal products and fat account for 70–80 percent of all cancers. The good news is that we can fight back. Adopting a healthy lifestyle dramatically lowers our risk.

AN ASSIGNMENT

Think about becoming a part-time vegetarian. Set aside at least one day a week for meals without meat and high-fat dairy products. As you become more experienced, gradually increase the number of meat-free meals you eat each week. Working toward the optimal diet is an important way to protect your health.

Disarming Diabetes

In times past a diagnosis of diabetes was somewhat akin to one of leprosy: Once you got it, it stuck around for the duration. And it brought along a lifetime of loathsome burdens.

No more! Today many people are beating diabetes. They are normalizing their blood sugars and getting off insulin by making healthful lifestyle changes.

What exactly is diabetes? And isn't it inherited?

Diabetes occurs when the body becomes unable to handle glucose (sugar), which builds up to dangerous levels in the blood. The problem revolves around insulin, a pancreatic hormone that enables body cells to use glucose and thus brings down high blood sugar levels.

There are two kinds of diabetes. Type I afflicts about 5 percent of diabetics. They are usually thin and rarely overweight. This type of diabetes is often hereditary, usually begins in childhood or youth and is commonly called *juvenile diabetes.* Since these diabetics cannot survive without insulin, it is now officially called *Insulin-Dependent Diabetes Mellitus* (IDDM).

Type II diabetes is different. Called "adult-onset diabetes," or *Non-Insulin-Dependent Diabetes Mellitus* (NIDDM), it afflicts an estimated sixteen million Americans. This type usually hits after age fifty as people get older and fatter. In contrast to the juvenile diabetics, most Type II diabetics, when diagnosed, have plenty of insulin in their bodies. But something blocks the insulin; it cannot do its job properly.

What causes Type II diabetes?

Studies demonstrate a strong relationship to fat—in the diet and on the body. The disease is rare in areas of the world where fat intake is low and obesity uncommon.

Most of the time the problem in adult-onset diabetes is not a defective pancreas that is unable to produce sufficient insulin, but a lack of sensitivity to insulin. This resistance of the cells to insulin appears to relate directly to obesity and to excess fat in the diet.

But isn't sugar the culprit?

James Anderson, MD, professor of medicine and clinical nutrition at the University of Kentucky Medical College and a respected authority on diabetes, evaluated the effect of diet composition on blood sugar levels. Just as others had done before him, Dr. Anderson was able to turn lean, healthy young men into mild diabetics in less than two weeks by feeding them a rich 65 percent fat diet. A similar group, fed a lean 10 percent fat diet plus one pound of sugar per day, did not produce even one diabetic after eleven weeks when the experiment was terminated.

So what's the best way to treat this disease?

Lowering the amount of fat, oil and grease in the diet plays a crucial role. When less fat is eaten, less fat reaches the bloodstream. This begins a complicated process, which gradually restores the cells' sensitivity to insulin, which can then facilitate the entry of sugar from the bloodstream into the body cells. The effect is often dramatic. A Type II diabetic who lowers daily fat intake down to 10–15 percent of total calories can often bring blood sugar levels to normal ranges in less than eight weeks. Many are eventually able to get off diabetic medication entirely—both pills and injections.

Eating more natural, fiber-rich foods plays an important role by helping stabilize blood sugar levels. When foods are eaten without their normal complement of fiber, blood sugar levels can quickly shoot up. Normally a surge of insulin counteracts this. People who consume refined foods, drinks and snacks high in calories but low in fiber may experience hikes and dips in blood sugar levels all day long. High-fiber foods, on the other hand, smooth out these blood sugar fluctuations and stabilize energy levels.

Active physical exercise has an insulin-like reaction in that it *burns up the fuel* (blood sugar and fatty acids) more rapidly.

Normalizing body weight is often all that is necessary to bring the blood sugar back to normal. The low-fat, high-fiber diet will greatly aid this effort, as will regular, active exercise.

What about Type I diabetes?

Insulin-dependent, or juvenile, diabetics will need to take insulin for life until pancreatic transplants become feasible and affordable. However, the high-fiber, low-fat diet will help reduce the amount of insulin required to maintain stable blood sugar levels and reduce the ever-present threat of vascular complications.

Today, a newborn baby who lives seventy years will have a one-in-five chance of becoming diabetic, if the present diabetic rate trends continue, according to the National Institutes of Health. But this need not be! The same lifestyle measures that are disarming and normalizing many cases of Type II diabetes are preventive as well. Start now. Beat diabetes before it happens!

How can I beat this needless suffering?

Diabetes is a leading cause of new blindness, foot and leg amputations and hearing impairment. The worst part is that many people suffer needlessly. The following chart gives you the formula that can help beat this disease:

How to Beat Diabetes (Type II)

1. Eat more natural fiber-rich foods, simply prepared, low in fats, grease and sugar. Freely use whole-grain products, tubers and legumes, salads and vegetables, and eat a substantial breakfast daily—a hot multi-grain cereal will curb your appetite for hours and stabilize your blood sugar.

2. Use fresh whole fruits, but not more than three servings a day (if you have diabetes).

3. Avoid refined and processed foods. They are usually high in fat and sugar and low in fiber.

4. Markedly reduce fats, oils and grease. If you use animal products, use them lean and very sparingly, more like a condiment. And watch oily and creamy dressings and sauces.

5. Walk briskly each day. Two thirty-minute walks every day are ideal to help burn up the extra sugar in your blood.

6. Work with a physician experienced in the effects of dietary therapy to monitor and adjust your insulin need.

CHAPTER SUMMARY

One in five people in North America develop diabetes at some point in their life, yet this disease can be prevented and even cured. Low fat, both in the diet and on the body, is the secret.

AN ASSIGNMENT

Make sure you are not adding unnecessary fat and oil to food when you cook. Keeping your meals lean helps keep you lean, too—and that's important if you want to stay free of diabetes.

Building Better Bones

Osteoporosis (literally, *porous bone*) is a disease that silently and painlessly weakens the bones of twenty-five million Americans. Previously sturdy bones gradually become thin and fragile, their interiors soft and spongy. As a result, bones break, giving rise to the term *brittle bones.*

Osteoporosis may cause as many as 1.3 million fractures a year. Hip fractures can be both disabling and deadly. Spinal fractures, on the other hand, are often painless, but can rob a person of two to eight inches of height. The resultant spinal curvature is the source of *dowager's hump.*

How can I tell if I have osteoporosis?

Without professional help, you can't—not until you fracture a bone or start shrinking in height, and that's very late in the progression of the disease. Earlier diagnosis is best done by a physician's testing at a reliable medical center.

If you are middle-aged or older, and have two or more of the following risk factors, you should be tested: sedentary lifestyle, early menopause, high-protein diet, chronic use of corticosteroids, low estrogen, or cigarettes, caffeine or alcohol use. Lean Caucasians and Asians are more susceptible than other races probably because they have smaller bones.

How does osteoporosis develop?

Normal bones continue to increase in strength and thickness until around age thirty-five. Then the process gradually reverses itself, and small amounts of bone are lost each year. This loss accelerates in women after menopause and can continue for seven to fifteen years. When risk factors are present, bone loss occurs even faster and osteoporosis may develop. Although usually considered a disease of older women, 20 percent of victims are men.

What can be done to treat this disease?

Several treatments are being used. Please consider the benefits and risks of each:

- *Hormone Replacement Therapy:* When used, it slows down bone loss, but increases the risk for heart disease, uterine and breast cancer, thrombophlebitis (blood clots) and gallbladder disease. It can aggravate diabetes and contribute to hypertension. Women also face the prospect of continuing menstrual periods and needing periodic uterine biopsies. In high-risk cases, however, the benefits may outweigh the risks.

- *Vitamin D:* The body uses vitamin D to absorb calcium, but most Americans get more than they need; additional supplements have not proven beneficial.

- *Fluoride:* It is used experimentally, but long-term results are controversial.

- *Calcium:* The World Health Organization recommends 500 mg of calcium a day. Various health organizations in North America recommend up to 1,000 mg a day. There is not sufficient documentation of calcium deficiency to be more specific about recommended intake.

- *Exercise:* Bones will not thicken and strengthen without regular, weight-bearing exercise, such as walking. To retain their minerals, bones *need* to be pressed, pushed, pulled and twisted against gravity.

- *A low-protein diet:* This is the most promising therapy on the horizon. The body uses calcium in its metabolism of excess protein and then flushes the calcium through the kidneys. Studies show that calcium is always lost from bones when animal protein intake is too high—regardless of how many calcium-rich foods one eats or how many calcium supplements one swallows.

What makes you think protein might be a culprit?

Eskimos in the far north consume diets extremely high in both protein (250–400 gm/day) and calcium (1,500–2,500 mg/day). In spite of their high calcium intake and the very active lives they lead, they have the highest rate of osteoporosis of any world population.

The Bantu tribes in Africa, on the other hand, consume an average of 50 grams of protein and less than 400 mg of calcium a day, predominantly from plant foods. Yet, even though Bantu women bear an average of ten children, making special demands on calcium reserves, they are essentially free of osteoporosis. In contrast, relatives of the Bantu who have migrated to the United States and adopted the American dietary lifestyle eventually experience a rate of osteoporosis comparable to that of the rest of the American population.

How about prevention?

Most populations around the world average 400 mg of calcium a day without any evidence of osteoporosis. It's strangely paradoxical that osteoporosis has become epidemic in the United States, where the consumption of calcium-rich dairy products and calcium supplements is the highest in the world.

North Americans eat two to three times more protein than they need. Reducing protein intake to the Recommended Daily Allowance of 50–60 grams a day, along with daily active exercise and a healthful diet low in salt and caffeine, holds promise of turning the tide in the battle against brittle bones.

The body "spends" calcium as it processes animal protein. When there is not enough calcium available in the diet, it "borrows" from another source—the bones.

With so much protein to be processed, it is almost impossible to get enough calcium to balance the loss. Slowly over the years the bones become brittle and weak.

The solution is not to take more calcium supplements, but to eat less animal protein. This allows the body to conserve the calcium already stored in the bones.

What are good sources of calcium and high-protein foods?

The following chart lists some typical sources of calcium. Notice how high they are in protein. With some of these foods you get a lot of calcium, but you lose even more as the body deals with the excess protein.

Calcium in Concentrated Protein Foods			
	Serving Size	Calcium (in mg)	Protein (in gm)
Beef, chicken	5 oz.	15	34–45
Cheese, cheddar	4 slices	900	35
Milk, whole	2 glasses	575	18

This chart also lists good sources of calcium. But please notice the moderate amounts of protein provided by these foods. An added bonus is that they are all low in fat and high in fiber.

Calcium in Unconcentrated Protein Foods			
	Serving size	Calcium (in mg)	Protein (in gm)
Collard greens	1 cup	360	5
Spinach, broccoli	1 cup	175	5
Bread	2 slices	50–90	5

Everyone knows that you can't save money when you spend more than you make. The same principle applies to calcium: You can't keep bones strong if you are flushing their calcium out with a diet high in animal protein, coupled with excessive salt and caffeine.

CHAPTER SUMMARY

Osteoporosis is epidemic in North America, even though the consumption of calcium-rich dairy products and supplements is the highest in the world. By reducing the intake of animal protein, salt and caffeine and by adopting a program of daily exercise, along with a nicotine-free lifestyle, the tide can be turned in the battle against this crippling disease.

AN ASSIGNMENT

Make an effort to cut down on calcium-robbing, high-protein meats and dairy products. Instead, look to low-protein sources of calcium found in whole grains and dark-green leafy vegetables.

Creeping Fat

A mericans, on the average, are heavier than the citizens of any other major nation. Obesity is one of our leading public health problems. So serious is this disease that thirty-six million people are at significant medical risk.

That's frightening. No wonder weight-loss diets *are so popular!*

Yes, and far too many people fall prey to fads and eating plans that offer quick results. Like a conditioned reflex, extra pounds spell D-I-E-T to most people. A recent survey found that 40–50 percent of Americans between the ages of thirty-five and fifty-nine were on some kind of diet at any given time.

The sad truth is that unless people make lasting changes in their lifestyles and consistently choose healthful foods on a regular basis, their efforts are largely wasted. Nearly 95 percent of dieters regain their lost weight within a year, usually with a bonus. Constantly losing and regaining weight is frustrating and demoralizing, and it does more damage than good.

Would it be better to just stay fat?

For many people, remaining overweight would be less harmful than endlessly playing the rhythm game of *girth control.* Before running up the white flag of surrender, however, take a careful look at the health risks of being overweight.

Extra weight shortens life. Recent reports indicate that as little as five to ten pounds increase mortality figures. It has been calculated that every extra pound shaves about one month from one's life span. Sixty pounds will cost five years!

Obesity, by definition, occurs when a person is 20 percent or more above ideal weight. Being 10–19 percent over ideal weight is usually termed *overweight.*

Excess weight lays the foundation for nearly every degenerative disease except osteoporosis. Obese people are three times more likely to have heart disease, four times more likely to suffer from high blood pressure, five times more likely to develop diabetes and elevated blood cholesterol, and six times more likely to have gallbladder disease.

They also develop more cancer of the colon, rectum, prostate, breast, cervix, uterus and ovaries, and they suffer more osteoarthritis and low back pain. Overweight people are like ticking bombs waiting for one or more of these diseases to explode in their lives.

In addition, extra weight affects self-image. In today's appearance-oriented society it can be a great psychological burden.

How do extra pounds harm the body?

The key to the problem is calories—too many of them. Overweight happens when you eat more calories than your body can use. Whether calories come from fat, protein, sugar or starch, the leftovers are turned into fat. Some of this fat floats around in the blood, plastering and gradually plugging vital oxygen-carrying arteries.

The rest of the leftover fat ends up in the body's central fat bank, located around the midsection. Embarrassing branch offices often pop up in other parts of the body. For every 3,500 excess calories received by the body, one pound of fat is placed on deposit.

Excess fat relates directly to health. A 10 percent weight *reduction* in men thirty-five to fifty-five years of age will result in a 20 percent decrease in coronary heart disease. On the other hand, a 10 percent *increase* in weight produces a 30 percent increase in coronary disease.

This is just one example of many such relationships. Every pound counts, one way or the other.

So what's the secret of lasting weight loss?

The simple strategy for successful weight control is threefold:

- *Increase* the quality and amount of food eaten while decreasing the number of calories.

- *Increase* the rate at which calories are burned by increasing physical activity and muscle size.

- Make the above two lifestyle practices a permanent part of life.

Begin by eating generous amounts of high-fiber foods, like whole grains, vegetables, fruits, potatoes, yams and beans. Omit as much fat and sugar from the diet as possible, as well as refined and processed foods and snacks. These things are stuffed with calories and have negligible nutrients. Use animal products such as meat, eggs, ice cream and cheese very sparingly. They have no fiber and are loaded with fat. This kind of eating plan, plus a brisk daily walk, will help you lose one to two pounds a week, without feeling deprived and hungry!

This sounds like the same advice for diseases like heart disease and stroke.

Over and over you've heard the same advice: Change your lifestyle to prevent heart disease, stroke, hypertension, diabetes and a host of other life-shortening diseases. Why do all these problems have the same solution? Because a low-fat, whole-foods diet is not a gimmick or fad—it's the diet your body was designed for. It should come as no surprise, then, that the same diet that keeps your arteries clean and reduces the risk of cancer also helps you lose weight—and keep it off for good.

Fats make fat. Ounce per ounce the American diet packs a lot of calories. That is because it is high in fat. Look at the comparison: A gram of fat contains more than twice the calories of an equal amount of protein or carbohydrate.

Calories per Gram

Fat	9
Alcohol	7
Carbohydrate (sugar, starch)	4
Protein	4

CHAPTER SUMMARY

Being overweight hurts your self-image and lays the foundation for many diseases. The secret of lasting weight loss begins with eating generous amounts of high-fiber foods while limiting animal products and refined foods. Combine this with a brisk, daily walk, and you will easily drop those extra pounds.

AN ASSIGNMENT

When you shop, check the labels to see how much fat, sugar and fiber the foods you buy contain. Choose those that are very low in calorie-dense fats and sugars, but high in fiber. Remember, if you eat products that carry most of their weight as fat, soon you will be doing the same.

Esau's Pottage

⅓ cup brown rice
1 cup sautéed onions
1 cup lentils
4 cups water
herbs to taste: marjoram, thyme, Mrs. Dash

Add ingredients to Crock-Pot and cook until tender. Add herbs shortly before serving. Garnish with parsley and slices of red bell pepper.

WEIGHT CONTROL

Myths and
Fads

Diets

Soft Drinks

Snacks

Exercise

Calories

Ideal Weight

Fail-Safe
Formula

When Success
Is an Illusion

T he appeal is all but irresistible. *Lose ten pounds in ten days—with a new, scientifically proven formula!* The struggling, discouraged, overweight person grasps for another straw. He needs to believe.

Weight loss is weight loss, isn't it? Does it matter how a person loses it?

Most people who lose weight believe they are losing fat; in reality they may be losing mostly water, plus muscle and other vital tissues.

Several years ago diet pills were popular. Many of them included a diuretic (water pill). Since the body is about 70 percent water, it is relatively easy for such pills to remove several pounds of water quickly. The scales look good—for a few days. But gradually the body balances itself by replacing the water, and there goes the weight loss.

An overdose of protein will accomplish basically the same result. The liver changes excess protein into *blood urea nitrogen* (BUN), which causes the kidneys to force water from the body. It takes much more water to wash out the products of excess protein metabolism than it does to take care of the breakdown products of either carbohydrates or fats.

Some quick-weight-loss diets take advantage of the fact that a high protein intake can cause spectacular weight loss in a short time. This is a dangerous practice, however. That's why such diets are usually physician-supervised and limited to short periods of time, normally about two weeks. The scales show gratifyingly low numbers, but most of the weight returns in a short time as the body replaces lost water.

Can I really lose weight on such a gradual diet?

Moderately overweight people usually lose one to two pounds a week on a well-balanced diet; seriously overweight persons may lose a little more. Slow, steady weight loss has many advantages over the radical diets:

- It does not throw the body into the mode of *starvation metabolism.*

- Binges and failures are much less frequent.

- Hunger becomes more manageable.

- Chances are good that the weight lost is really fat.

But perhaps the most important aspect of slower weight loss is that *it allows time to establish new and more healthful habits of eating.* A person must develop a lifestyle that is consistent with maintaining the new weight if the weight loss is to have any chance of being permanent.

I'm desperate to lose weight; I have no patience with slow programs. Wouldn't quick weight loss be better than none at all?

Losing and regaining weight, over and over, is one of the most harmful things you can do to your body. The truth is that remaining overweight would be less harmful to overall health than this yo-yo effect. Repeated weight loss through crash diets, followed by regaining the weight, gradually depletes muscle tissue and adds fat tissue. And because muscle tissue is where fat is burned, you will become increasingly unable to lose weight.

Of even more concern are the psychological consequences. Enduring years of repeated failure and humiliation produces emotional scars that often remain for a lifetime. People seduced by the magic of quick weight loss offered by the merchants of misery do shed pounds initially, but they almost invariably end up weighing more than they did before.

This is not to minimize the fact that overweight persons carry increased health risks. They have more heart disease, hypertension, diabetes, gallbladder disease and cancer than do people of normal weight. They also die sooner.

Don't become a slave to the scale, checking it daily for immediate results to problems that took years to develop. Get started on a healthful program. And be patient. It's the long haul that matters. The illusions will fade, but the eventual rewards will be solid and lasting.

What is the right way to lose weight?

Through moderate exercise (walking) and eating a well-balanced diet of low-fat, high-fiber foods, you can lose one to two pounds a week. That might not get you slim in time for summer, but it is a sensible health-conscious approach to successful long-term weight control.

How does fiber help?

One of the many virtues of fiber is that it acts as a safety mechanism to keep you from overeating. It helps you feel full before you can eat too many calories.

Fiberless foods lack this automatic shut-off. By the time you feel full, you've eaten enough calories for a family of five. Will power is the only thing that stands between you and obesity—and we all know how effective that is.

What are low-fiber foods?

All animal products lack fiber. That includes meat, milk, eggs and cheese.

Processing mills and refines the fiber out of many other foods as well. Sugar, white flour, oils and most packaged foods fall into this category.

Corn oil is a good example of this process. It takes fourteen ears of corn to make one tablespoon of oil. Imagine trying to eat fourteen ears of corn at one sitting. Impossible! Yet it is easy to sit down and eat many tablespoons of oil in the form of salad dressings or margarine.

CHAPTER SUMMARY

Diets that promise to help you lose weight quickly are suspect. They use tricks that make you weigh less, but they often have no lasting effect.

Moderately overweight people can usually lose one to two pounds a week on a well-balanced program of healthy eating and exercise. That's the wise way to take (and keep) weight off.

AN ASSIGNMENT

Fruits, vegetables, whole grains and legumes are high in fiber. Eat them in abundance. Start with this low-fat, high-fiber soup. Serve it with hearty, whole-wheat bread and a salad. Eat all you want. You will fill up long before you fatten up.

Split Pea Soup

1 cup split peas	6 cups water
1 cup sautéed onions	¼ cup barley
1 bay leaf	1 potato, chopped
½ tsp. thyme	1 carrot, chopped
1 celery stalk, chopped	½ Tbsp. sweet basil

Add peas, water, onions, barley and bay leaf to Crock-Pot; cook until "almost" tender. Add remaining ingredients, and cook another 45–60 minutes. Add water if necessary. Leftovers can be used as a spread for bread or as a topping on baked potatoes.

Serves 6.

The Quick-Fix Trap

We spend billions of dollars every year on diets and weight control paraphernalia, yet the results are dismal. For many, permanent, successful weight control is more difficult to achieve than victory over drugs, tobacco or alcohol.

Would it be better to stop trying? To just stay fat?

Yes, it would be safer to remain obese than to jump from one diet fad to another, lose pounds now, and gain them back later. Research shows that this yo-yo effect gradually depletes important body tissues such as muscle and bone. Eventually it weakens the body so that it becomes more susceptible to disease and less able to shed excess fat.

But isn't it dangerous to remain overweight?

Being fat isn't healthful. Excess weight impairs health and shortens life. As little as ten to fifteen pounds of extra weight produces measurable changes that can lay the foundation for degenerative disease. And, as we have mentioned, for every ten pounds of overweight, a life span can be shortened by as much as a year.

So what is the answer?

People who are overweight need major revisions in thinking and attitudes. The scenario played out in millions of lives goes something like this: a few weeks on the latest wonder diet; have the jaws wired; take a series of shots or pills; check into a fat farm. And presto, down goes the weight! Celebration! New clothes!

But within days after finishing their "program," these people resume their former eating patterns and lifestyle. In a few weeks or months the lost pounds are back, often with a bonus.

Weight control programs usually fail because they are short-term fixes for long-term problems. It is time to face the reality that obesity can be a serious and life-threatening condition.

OK, I'm convinced. What must I do?

Managing obesity is much more than a dietary problem. Like diabetes, hypertension, alcoholism or smoking, obesity requires a comprehensive approach to lifestyle changes. Follow these guidelines for good eating and you will conquer the problem:

You have to have a long-term commitment. A lifelong commitment does not change when binges or other serious lapses occur. With this kind of commitment, you can get up when you fall, start again and persevere.

You need to identify and change habits that cause obesity. This may be as simple as eliminating soft drinks or cutting back on fats and oils. Or it may require you to completely restructure your eating patterns and lifestyle.

Changing lifelong habits is among the most difficult things a person can do, and the process is very threatening. Faithful, regular meetings with a support group greatly increase the chances of success. This kind of team effort is almost a *must* for those more than twenty pounds overweight or who have had problems several years.

Attitudes often need radical surgery. Willingness to change is critically important. Read books, attend seminars, join fitness groups and make friends with health-minded people. Weight control is not a vanity trip. Keep the focus on improved health, and the weight will take care of itself.

Look for a weight-control plan that is consistent with a lifetime of good health. This will include regular exercise, a low-fat, high-fiber diet and a physical, mental and psychological outlook that meets your needs in every area of life. Weight control should be only part of a full and fulfilling life—not its main preoccupation.

Such a workable life plan is possible. Many have succeeded. Put your heart into it and keep it there.

Take the long-term approach. It is virtually impossible to lose weight and keep it off if you don't modify your lifestyle. Diets are a short-term solution to a long-term problem. That is why nearly 95 percent of all dieters regain their lost weight within a year.

Make eating the right foods a permanent part of your daily life. This is the solution to weight control. You can beat the bulge and live a happier, healthier life.

CHAPTER SUMMARY

Diets are quick-fix traps that don't last. Many people skip from one to the next, losing weight now and gaining it back later. This cycle is discouraging, defeating and often dangerous. A lifetime commitment to good health practices is the only safe path to permanent weight control.

AN ASSIGNMENT

Can you make the commitment?

Turn inward for a moment. Can you make a long-term commitment to this style of eating? Are you willing to bypass the seductive offers of diets that claim to "melt the pounds off" in favor of a focus on good health?

Be honest with yourself. Give the part of you that wants to eat only chocolate as much of a voice as the part that promises never to eat anything "bad" again. Recognize that each voice is an extreme that exists in all of us. Lasting change happens somewhere in the middle, and it doesn't happen overnight. It is a growth process in which new behaviors and values gradually replace old ones. Answer the question now. Use an extra sheet of paper if necessary.

A Carbonated
Generation

A mericans now consume twice as many sodas as they did twenty-
five years ago—a habit that contributes to overweight, tooth
decay and the loss of bone mass. We now average two soft drinks per day
for every man, woman and child in this country.

Aren't soft drinks a good way to help people drink more fluids?

Take one glass of water, add 8–12 teaspoons of sugar, mix in a dose
of chemicals—and you'll get a soft drink.

The extra sugar intake from soft drinks produces at least five unde-
sirable side effects:

1. *Unbalanced nutrition.* Most soft drinks contain 120–180 calories of sugar, but no needed nutrients. A typical sedentary
   woman requires only about 1,200–1,600 total calories a day
   to maintain optimal weight and good health. Two or three
   soft drinks can considerably reduce her daily food allotment
   as well as her nutrient supply. Over time, this imbalance
   could cause her nutritional status to become marginal.

   The same applies to sedentary men who need about
   1,800–2,400 calories a day.

2. *Extra fat storage.* If the soft drink calories are *added* to the food calories, the excess will be stored as fat.

3. *Uneven blood sugar.* Sugar calories lack fiber and rapidly enter the blood stream, raising blood sugar levels and providing a temporary boost of energy. When the blood sugar level goes up, insulin enters the bloodstream to pull the raised blood sugar back down, and energy levels drop. This sequence promotes the cycle of reaching for another, and yet another, soft drink or other sugary snack.

4. *Delayed digestion.* When a sugared drink arrives in a stomach that is processing other food, digestion slows down until the new calories are handled. An occasional drink probably wouldn't make much difference, but if it happens several times a day, it can prolong digestion and stress the stomach.

5. *Acid rebound.* Most beverages, including sodas, increase acid secretion in the stomach. This increase usually occurs after the beverage leaves the stomach, producing a *rebound* effect.

No wonder diet drinks have become so popular! Is this a good solution?

Diet drinks solve the sugar problems, but that's not the whole story. Most beverages, sugared or not, contain preservatives, flavorings, colorings and other such chemicals. Some of these substances need to be detoxified and eliminated from the body. They may also irritate sensitive stomach linings.

What, then, is the safest way to meet body fluid needs?

Water is the perfect beverage. It has no calories, requires no digestion, does not irritate and is exactly what the body needs to carry on the life processes. How much should we drink? We should drink enough to keep the urine pale—about six to eight glasses of water daily.

What are you drinking? Sometimes it is eye opening to find out. Listed below are some beverages you might consume. Try to estimate how many of each you drink during a typical week. Then, for each type of beverage, multiply the number consumed by the number of calories it contains. Write this in the totals column. When you are done, add all the totals to get your grand total.

My Beverage Pattern			
Drink (standard serving)	**Calories**	**Number**	**Total**
Coffee, cream & sugar	75		
Orange juice	110		
Soda, juice, punch	140		
Nonfat milk	90		
Whole milk	160		
Milk shake	425		
Beer	150		
Cocktail or mixed drink	150		
Mineral water	0		
Water	0		
Total Calories		**Grand Total**	

It takes 3,500 excess calories to make one pound of fat. Assuming you eat enough to maintain your weight, how many days would it take you to *drink on* an extra pound?

You can calculate this by dividing 3,500 by the number of calories you get from beverages each day. For example, if you drank one beer and two coffees, the calculation would be:

Total calories for one beer and two coffees = 300;
3,500/300 = 11.6 days.

In other words, it would take just under twelve days to add an extra pound of fat. At that rate you could gain thirty pounds a year just from what you drink!

Now it is your turn. Take your weekly grand total from the previous exercise. Then divide it into 3,500 to see how long it takes you to drink an extra pound's worth of calories. Fill in the blanks below:

Number of Days to Drink 3,500 Calories

3,500 ÷ daily calories you drink _____ = _____ days.

Water is the way to go. If you are serious about controlling your weight, it would be wise to eliminate those sneaky liquid calories. Stop the sodas, lose the liquor, shelve the shakes. Water is what your body needs and craves.

CHAPTER SUMMARY

North Americans, on average, drink more soft drinks than they do water. That means they are getting a lot of calories but not much nutrition. Drinking calorie-loaded beverages is one sure recipe for gaining weight. Switch to water—it's the slender person's drink of choice.

AN ASSIGNMENT

Cut calories by drinking more water and fewer high-calorie beverages. If you don't like the taste of tap water, add a twist of lemon or buy bottled water. The more water you drink, the less likely you are to reach for other beverages. That alone will cut calories and help stabilize your weight.

A Nation of Grazers

Americans spend $10 billion a year on salted snack foods such as potato chips, pork rinds, popcorn and the like. And we spend at least that much more on sweet snacks.

We need snacks, don't we? I read somewhere that it is difficult to get all the nutrients a person needs without snacks.

That bit of wisdom came out of a study done on children. It holds up only when children don't get nourishing, well-balanced meals, or when they aren't hungry enough at mealtime to eat the calories they need.

Most Americans, children or adults, have no real idea what it is like to be hungry. From birth, kids are fed almost constantly. The habit carries on through the years. We have become a nation of *grazers.*

But "grazing" is supposed to be a good way to lose weight! You eat a little every hour or so, all day. That way, you don't get hungry, so you don't overeat.

Actually, the calories gained from snacks and beverages can add up to more calories than some people should eat all day!

Suppose, for instance, you have a mid-morning snack of coffee with cream and sugar and a jelly doughnut.

Add a mid-afternoon snack of a soft drink and a candy bar, plus a late afternoon snack of a cup of coffee with cream and sugar and three cookies.

Top it off in the evening with a typical TV snack: a soft drink, ten potato chips and five cheese crackers. If this sounds familiar, you'd better watch out—all that snacking added about 1,500 calories to your day! Now you know why the old saying is still true: *The bigger the snacks, the bigger the slacks.* As a matter of fact, many people have gained control of their weight simply by cutting out snacking.

Are you saying that we don't need snacks?

Yes. The snack habit is just that, *a habit.* With regular, adequate meals there will be much less need for snacks.

What's more, people have fewer digestive problems when they eat simple meals of mostly high-fiber plant foods and then allow their stomachs to rest for awhile. Ideally, meals should be spaced about four to five hours apart.

Warning: Snacking can be hazardous.

Stop for a moment and think of the foods you snack on. Do you reach for a juicy apple, or do you unwrap a candy bar? Do you munch raw vegetables, or tear into a sack of chips? Most people opt for high-sugar, high-fat or high-salt goodies to get them from one meal to the next. The extra pounds they wear testify to their devotion.

Any suggestions for a "must-have-a-snack" attack?

Drink a big glass of water. It has no calories and requires no digestion. It passes right through, giving everything a good rinse.

If you must have more, eat a piece of fresh fruit or a handful of raw veggies.

The best way to fight off a *snack attack,* however, is to remember that the calories you save by shunning those snacks will gradually melt off unwanted bulges. While it may not always be true to say, *"Once on the lips, forever on the hips,"* there's no more doubting the fact, *"The bigger the snacks, the bigger the slacks."*

If you want to lose weight, you must deal with that snack habit. Here are some hints to help you make the change:

Start with a good breakfast. Beating the snack habit begins with a hearty breakfast. It should provide plenty of unrefined complex carbo-hydrates for lasting energy. Let whole grains, which are high in these carbohydrates, form the core of the meal. Eat plenty, until you are full.

Building a Hearty Breakfast

Cereals—cooked 7-grain cereal, waffles, granola
Skim milk or dairy substitutes
Fresh fruit—all types, bananas, citrus and melon
Additional fruit—fresh or frozen
Bread—whole-wheat or multi-grain

Watch out for triggers. Many habits, snacking included, are linked to signals from your environment. For example, you might get the urge for a candy bar whenever you pass that vending machine at work. Or there might be a certain television commercial that makes you want to open a bag of chips. What triggers your urge to snack?

Develop alternate behaviors. How do you fight a snack attack? Do other things to disrupt the pattern. If you are bogged down in your work and need a boost, go for a quick walk to the corner and back. Drink a glass of water rather than the usual soda. If you must eat some-thing, try a piece of fruit or some raw vegetables.

CHAPTER SUMMARY

The calories you get from snacking can add up to an extra meal—a big one at that. Many people are able to control their weight just by kicking the snack habit. You can, too, by eating adequate meals high in unre-fined complex carbohydrates and fiber. These meals will provide you with steady energy you need to make it from one meal to the next.

AN ASSIGNMENT

Start your mornings with a hearty breakfast, and skip the mid-morning goodies. Together, these habits will help you look good and feel better.

Walk Out
of Obesity

In America today, fitness is *in*. Strut your sweat. Lace up your Reeboks. Flaunt your leotards. The majority of Americans, woefully unfit, are feeling out of step.

When I hear that a person has to run ten miles to work off an ice cream sundae, I feel like—"What's the use!"

There are other choices. You can burn the calories by sleeping for fifteen hours or by watching TV for twelve hours. The problem, of course, is that there aren't enough hours in the day to *sleep away* an ice cream sundae along with your other meals. That's why exercise is so important. It helps your body burn calories faster.

The body is a motor that runs all the time. The rate at which the body motor idles is called its *basal metabolic rate* (BMR). The faster the motor runs, the more fuel is used.

However, when fuel supplies are cut (not enough calories consumed), an inner mechanism turns down the body's idling speed. Available fuel now burns more slowly. This function is life-saving under conditions of starvation, but it defeats the person trying to lose weight.

Can this reaction be prevented?

Activity speeds up the body's metabolic rate. Not only are more calories burned during exercise, but the effect continues for several hours. That's why most people feel more energetic when they exercise. The BMR of the body reflects this. A regular exercise program promotes weight loss by pepping up the metabolism—burning calories faster.

How many calories do I need?

Multiplying your current weight by ten approximates the daily calories you would need to maintain the status quo if you are bedfast—this is your BMR. Most people use an additional 30 percent of their BMR calories for activity calories. Added together, this figure represents the number of calories you must eat every day to maintain your weight.

If you are fairly sedentary and weigh 150 pounds, for example, your BMR needs would be 1,500 calories, and your activity calories would be 450, for a total of 1,950 calories.

To *lose* weight, you need to reduce the number of calories you eat or increase the number of calories you burn. When you develop a negative energy balance, you force your body to burn its reserve fuel, that is, fat.

Doesn't muscle tissue turn into fat as a person gets older?

Muscle tissue does *not* turn to fat. It is physiologically impossible for this to happen.

When people become less active, however, their muscles shrink and their BMR slows down. Eating habits often are not adjusted to this lessened activity, so as excess calories accumulate, the body stores the fat in numerous places, including the spaces around the muscle fibers.

An important point to understand is that the *muscles burn fat.* When more muscle tissue is present, fat will burn faster and more efficiently. On the other hand, lack of exercise and overly rigorous dieting will cause the body to *lose* muscle. If this situation persists for a long time, it may become almost impossible to lose further weight.

Is thirty minutes of exercise, three times a week, enough?

Once a person has reached normal weight and a good level of fitness, that may be sufficient. But people who are unfit and people who need to lose weight must aim higher—work toward an hour a day.

What is the best exercise?

The safest and best exercise is walking; swimming is a close second. People with higher levels of fitness may choose more strenuous exercises.

Start slowly with what you can do. How fast you go isn't the most important thing. What counts is the total distance covered and the duration of the activity. Some people must start with only five minutes at a time several times a day. A person who walks five minutes, carrying fifty pounds of extra weight, will burn more calories than a person carrying only twenty extra pounds who walks the same distance.

If you want to be thin, get in shape. Put your best foot forward, begin to walk your way out of obesity, and keep going for a lifetime!

Review the last three sections of this chapter, then answer these questions:

1. How much time a day should an overweight person spend exercising?

_____

2. What is the safest and best exercise?

_____

The answers to these questions are important because together they make up the second element of an effective weight-loss program: *exercise.*

Fortunately, this program can be gentle. You don't need to pump iron or run marathons. Just get yourself some comfortable walking shoes and step out the front door.

What if I don't have time to exercise?

Everyone is rushed these days. Even kids and retirees have full calendars. A half-hour of exercise every day can seem like an impossible dream.

Many busy people get their exercise out of the way by getting up a little earlier. Some walk during their lunch hour or at break times. Others like to unwind by walking in the evening after work. Be creative, and you will find that there is always time for a high-priority activity like exercise.

Of course there will be some days when you can't complete your whole exercise routine.When that happens, shoot for a shorter walk. A jaunt to the end of the street or around the house is better than no exercise at all. Don't strive for perfection and give up when you don't achieve it. Persistence is far more valuable than perfection when it comes to building a healthful lifestyle.

Share it with a friend. One of the best things about walking is you don't need to do it alone. Walking with others encourages communication. Many couples find it strengthens their relationship, and friends enjoy a companionship that makes the miles fly by.

CHAPTER SUMMARY

A regular exercise program helps you lose weight by boosting your metabolism. This causes you to burn more calories even when you are not exercising. It also increases your energy and endurance and lifts your spirits. Exercise is a high-yield investment.

AN ASSIGNMENT

Make walking a part of each day. Start with just ten minutes a day, and work up from there. When combined with a proper diet, walking is an effective way to keep your weight under control.

Building Caloric Bombs

We often take healthful, nutritious foods and turn them into caloric bombs. It's easy. It's insidious. And we do it without thinking.

Take an apple, for instance. It has vitamins, minerals, fiber and only 75–100 calories. If we ate apples as they come from the tree, we would have no problem. But we love to douse them with sugar and make applesauce, doubling the calories. Or we squeeze out the juice, removing most of the fiber and concentrating the calories. Even more popular is apple pie, an American special ranked along with motherhood, the flag and baseball. It is also a nutritional disaster—one slice *à la mode* can easily pack 500 calories.

I could eat a lot of apples for those calories!

That's the point. You would have to eat five or six apples to reach that caloric level. And you know you wouldn't do that. You would feel exceptionally full after two or three.

Or take the potato. By itself the lowly spud is a wonderfully nutritious food. How good is it? Well, a few years ago a scientist tried an experiment. He ate nothing but potatoes for a whole year. Surprisingly, he remained in good heath with plenty of energy.

But look at the way we eat potatoes today. A big 8-ounce potato, by itself, contains about 140 calories. But who eats a plain potato? Here are some of the things we do to dress it up:

Adding Calories to Your Potato

Potato	Calories
Plain potato (8 oz.)	140
With sour cream and butter	420
As hashbrowns	520
As french fries	530
As potato chips	1,200
Pringles	1,360

And that's just the tip of the iceberg. Fresh salads are doused with oily dressings. Most of our fruit goes into juices or pies, or it is canned in heavy syrup. Even when we cook fresh vegetables, we usually butter them or add a sauce, which can double and triple the calories. No wonder people have weight problems!

How can we go about reversing this trend?

The solutions are relatively simple. Food preferences, after all, are not inborn—they are learned and cultivated. They can be changed. Substituting a good habit and repeating it over and over with persistence and determination will do the trick.

You can begin by eating more natural foods that have been simply prepared. This includes choosing whole-grain products such as whole-wheat bread, whole-grain cereals, brown rice and pasta. It also includes eating fresh vegetables of all kinds. Tubers like potatoes and yams, and legumes like beans, peas and lentils are excellent choices.

Indulge yourself with fruit. Whenever possible, eat fresh, whole fruit without added sugar. Peeling and eating an orange, for example, gives you more food value and fiber than drinking juice, and it fills you up with fewer calories.

When food is eaten as grown, it is full of fiber and quite low in calories. By leaving those *caloric bombs* alone, at least most of the time, you can actually eat a larger quantity of food, feel full and satisfied— and still lose weight.

How many calories do I need?

Have you ever wondered how many calories you can eat before your body begins storing the excess as fat? To find out, start by calculating how many calories your body needs to keep you alive over a twenty-four-hour period.

Your basal metabolic rate (BMR for short) is the rate at which your body would burn calories if you decided to lie in bed all day. You can estimate that total by multiplying your weight by ten.

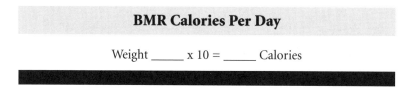

BMR Calories Per Day

Weight _____ x 10 = _____ Calories

Now, if you don't have an exercise program or engage in heavy labor, you burn an amount equal to 30 percent of your BMR calories as activity calories. For example, if your BMR calories totaled 1,500, you would burn an additional 450 calories as activity calories. Calculate your activity calories by multiplying your BMR calories by 0.3.

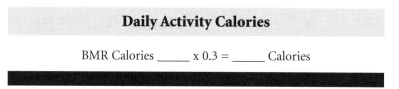

Daily Activity Calories

BMR Calories _____ x 0.3 = _____ Calories

The final step is to add your BMR and activity calories to get the number of calories you burn in a day. If you eat more than this number of calories, your body deposits the excess as fat. If you eat less, your body uses fat from its stores, and you lose weight.

Calories You Burn Daily

BMR _____ + Activity _____ = _____ Calories

It would be hard to exceed your calorie limit on the Optimal Diet because whole foods are high in fiber and low in fat. But when you start adding fat, watch out! Look what happens to this meal:

EXPLODING EMPTY FAT CALORIES

Food	Cal.		Added Fat	Cal.	Total Calories
Lettuce and Tomato Salad	40	+	Roquefort Dressing	160	200
Whole-Wheat Bread (1 slice)	65	+	Butter	70	135
Broccoli (½ cup)	35	+	Cheese Sauce	130	165
Vegetarian Entree or Broiled Fish (6 oz.)	220	+	Tartar Sauce	100	320
Large Baked Potato with Salsa	135	+	Sour Cream and Butter	180	315
Skim Milk (1 glass)	90	or	Whole Milk		160
Baked Apple with Date or Walnut	100	or	Apple Pie à la mode (⅙)		480
Total Calories	**685**		**Total Calories**		**1,775**

CHAPTER SUMMARY

We are not born with our appetites; they are habits we develop. By reeducating ourselves to avoid caloric bombs and to enjoy more natural, low-fat foods, we can eat more, feel full—and still lose weight.

An Assignment

Avoid caloric bombs. Work to reduce the oils, butters, dressings and gravies you add to your food. It is time to shift the scales in your favor!

The Right Weight Debate

I'm not obese," said one comedian. "I'm just short for my weight!" Whether short or tall, few people are happy about what they weigh.

How can I tell if I'm FIT or FAT?

A person's weight is a highly individual issue, but here are some guidelines. By definition, obese means being 20 percent or more above one's ideal weight. A person with an ideal weight of 120 pounds would be obese at 144 pounds or more. Overweight, on the other hand, means being 10–19 percent above one's ideal weight. Our hypothetical person with an ideal weight of 120 pounds would be overweight at 132–143 pounds.

How is your "ideal" weight determined?

Ideal weight can be set in several different ways. One way is to look at the records of large life insurance companies who are interested in finding predictors of longevity. They have discovered that certain ideal weight-to-height relationships correlate well with optimum life expectancy. The massive actuarial data of the Metropolitan Life Insurance Company formed the basis of its gender-specific Table of Desirable Weight, based on height and bone size.

Ideal Weights for Adults According to Frame

Height (No Shoes)	MEN Small Frame	Medium Frame	Large Frame	Height (No Shoes)	WOMEN Small Frame	Medium Frame	Large Frame
5'2"	115-123	121-133	129-144	4'10"	96-104	101-113	109-125
4"	121-129	127-139	135-152	5'0"	102-110	107-119	115-131
6"	128-137	134-147	142-161	2"	108-116	113-126	121-138
8"	136-145	142-156	151-170	4"	114-123	120-135	129-146
10"	144-154	150-165	159-179	6"	122-131	128-143	137-154
6'0"	152-162	158-175	168-189	8"	130-140	136-151	145-163
2"	160-171	167-185	178-199	10"	138-148	144-159	153-173
4"	168-179	177-195	187-209				

Metropolitan Life Insurance Height/Weight Table (1959)+ (Weight in lbs.)*

*Includes one pound for ordinary indoor clothing.
+Many established researchers consider the 1959 table of the Metropolitan Life Insurance Company more consistent with good health than the revised 1983 table with its higher values.

How is bone size calculated?

Although most people have a pretty good idea of their frame size, wrist and sometimes ankle measurements provide a more reliable method. In general, a wrist measurement for women of 5¼ inches or less is considered small-boned, between 5¼ to 6 inches is medium, and over 6 inches is large. For men, anything under 6 inches is small and anything over 7 inches is large.

Is there a simpler way to calculate ideal weight?

Here is a time-honored rule of thumb:

- For men—allow 100 pounds for 5 feet of height. For each additional inch, add 6 pounds. The ideal weight for a man 5 feet 10 inches tall would therefore be 160 pounds.

- For women—allow 106 pounds for 5 feet of height, but add 5 pounds for each additional inch. For a woman that is 5 feet 5 inches tall, that comes to 131 pounds. Large-boned men and women should add 5 percent to these figures.

Some athletes I know would flunk that test!

That's right, and that's why it's only a rule of thumb. Football players, for instance, have more muscle and greater muscle density than the average person. At the same time they carry very little fat. For this reason, the most accurate way to measure body fat is through hydrostatic (under water) weighing. Fat is buoyant and weighs less under water. This difference allows for calculations of what percentage of a person's body is composed of fat.

Where can I get weighed under water?

Look for places that advertise health screening tests. Some of them have tanks of water for this purpose. Others use swimming pools. However, this is an inconvenient and complicated process.

A simpler, more practical test is the *pinch test.* Trained health professionals use calipers to measure the thickness of skin folds at different places on the body. With the proper tables, they can then calculate body fat percentages with fair accuracy.

Can I do a pinch test on myself?

You can do a simplified pinch test yourself. Reach over to your left side, just below the last rib, and pull the skin and fat away from the underlying muscle. Hold it between your thumb and index finger and squeeze. If the space between your thumb and finger is more than three-fourths of an inch, you're in trouble!

CHAPTER SUMMARY

Knowing your ideal weight is important. Studies show that people who remain near this target live longer, healthier lives. Find out how close (or far) you are from your ideal weight.

AN ASSIGNMENT

A support network can keep you going when you feel like giving up. Find someone else interested in losing weight. Working together will make reaching your goals twice as easy—and twice as enjoyable.

Eat More, Weigh Less

E very second adult in the United States is overweight. Despite thirty years of increasingly sophisticated diets, the average person is now ten pounds heavier.

That sounds pretty grim. Is there a brighter side?

Actually, there's a Mr. or Ms. Goodweight inside each one of us—it may just be stuck behind layers of discouragement, bulges of overindulgence and mounds of misconceptions. We need to locate that special person inside and begin restoring the health, energy and self-confidence that's been buried far too long.

How do you do that?

By finding a lifestyle that maintains health, increases energy, lowers the risk of disease, reduces food bills and allows people to eat as much as they want and still lose weight without feeling hungry.

Surely that's an impossible dream!

Not really. Obesity occurs when calories eaten exceed the calories used by the body for physical activity and maintenance of its functions. These leftover calories are stored as fat. By the time 3,500 extra calories have accumulated, one pound of fat will have been deposited.

Adding an extra pat of butter (100 calories) to the daily diet will total up to ten extra pounds of body fat in one year! On the other hand, omitting a typical 500-calorie dessert for seven days will remove one pound of body fat. The secret to success lies in finding a way to eat fewer calories instead of eating less food.

That sounds like a contradiction!

Today's world is full of contradictions. Popular magazines and TV screens brim with beautiful, slender people—and with full-color ads of rich, fattening foods. Supermarkets offer 25,000 slickly packaged, calorie-dense products, along with magazines touting the latest quickie diet. Fast-food restaurants tempt from nearly every street corner with *takeout* service—while nutrition is what they take out!

Modern food technology has turned inexpensive, low-calorie, high-volume foods into expensive, high-calorie, low-volume *caloric bombs.* It's now possible to eat a whole meal's worth of calories with only a few bites of food. No wonder people feel hungry and dissatisfied—and overeat!

How does it happen? *Processing* strips seven pounds of sugar beets of their bulk, fiber and nutrients, producing one pound of *pure sugar.* Sugar and other refined sweeteners now account for about 20 percent of daily calories eaten.

Almost 50 percent of the modern Western diet consists of processed and concentrated calories devoid of vital nutrients and valuable fiber—a sure-fire formula for overweight.

So how do I go about losing weight?

If you love food but want to lose weight, then eat more:

- Fresh and steamed vegetables, but go easy on sauces and salad dressings

- Whole grains—cooked cereals, brown rice, whole-grain breads, pasta

- Tubers and other vegetables—potatoes, yams, squash and all kinds of beans, lentils and peas

- Fresh, whole fruits

These *foods as grown* are filling, nutritious, inexpensive and low in calories.

Eat less:

- Refined, processed and concentrated foods. They are high in calories and price and low in nutrients and fiber.

- Nuts, meats and rich dairy products. While these foods are nutritious, they have little fiber and bulk and are very high in fat and calories. Meats and cheeses, for instance, are 60–80 percent fat.

SECTION REVIEW

This chapter is the last of nine units devoted to weight control. As you have worked through them, we have encouraged you to try many new behaviors. Now that you have had a chance to experiment, we hope you will make them a permanent part of your life. Here they are in review:

Eight Steps to Permanent Weight Control

1. Read labels carefully and choose foods low in fat and less refined.

2. Build your diet around fruits, vegetables, grains, legumes and other "as grown" foods.

3. Make the Optimal Diet (page 237) your diet.

4. Make water your drink of choice. Avoid high-calorie beverages.

5. Kick the snack habit. Begin each day with a hearty breakfast that makes mid-morning snacking unnecessary.

6. Make exercise a part of your routine. Walk every day.

7. Reduce the oils, butters, dressings and other fats you add to foods.

8. Develop a support network with others who share your interest in making positive lifestyle changes.

For most of us, getting permanent control of a ballooning waistline requires a radical shift in diet. The table below summarizes the food selection principles we have presented:

Food Selection Principles

Eat freely from the following:

- Fruits—All fresh fruit (avocado and olives sparingly)

- Vegetables—All vegetables, greens, squash, tomatoes

- Legumes—All beans, peas, lentils, garbanzos

- Tubers—Potatoes, yams, sweet potatoes

- Grains—All whole grains, breads, pastas

Eat sparingly from the following:

- Nuts

- Flesh foods, if you insist—Small amounts (3 ounces no more than three times a week). Skinless fowl, fish fillet, lean beef.

Optional:

- Dairy—Nonfat milk, plain yogurt, skim-milk cheeses, buttermilk and low-fat cottage cheese in moderation.

- Eggs—Whites only. Substitute two egg whites for one egg in recipes.

CHAPTER SUMMARY

It is possible to eat as much as you want and still lose weight. The secret is knowing which foods to eat and which to avoid. The whole plant foods that promote good health and prevent disease are also ideal for taking weight off and keeping it off—for good.

AN ASSIGNMENT

This week is a time to integrate everything you have found helpful in the last eight lessons. You can release the thin person inside of you and enjoy a happier, healthier life.

UNDERSTANDING FOOD

Starch

Sugar

Bread

Protein

Milk

Meat

Fat

Cholesterol

Fiber

Salt

Vitamins and
Minerals

A New Superstar

S tarchy foods, long shunned as *fattening,* are the new superstars of the food galaxy. Today's news is that the road to better health is paved with potatoes, pasta, rice, beans and bread.

What about protein? Everyone needs protein!

Yes, but not so much. For a long time people assumed that because muscles are predominantly protein, we needed to eat a lot of it to be strong.

But the body is like a car. Once the car is built, only a few additional parts are needed here and there for maintenance. Similarly, a human adult needs relatively little protein for daily maintenance—around 44–61 grams per day. That's about 2 ounces of pure protein a day.

What the car does need on a regular basis is good clean gasoline. And carbohydrates are the *gasoline* of the body, the high-octane fuel that keeps it running smoothly.

Isn't fat also a body fuel?

Fat, in general, is stored fuel, carried as baggage. It is the *reserve tank.* If the body runs out of carbohydrate fuel it can dig out the spare stuff. But fat doesn't burn as cleanly as carbohydrates, and it's not as energy efficient.

What are carbohydrates?

Carbohydrates are the sugars and starches in the foods we eat. A lot of people don't understand the relationship between sugars and starches, and the confusion is compounded when terms like *simple carbohydrates* and *complex carbohydrates* are used.

In general, *simple carbohydrates* are the sugars and *complex carbohydrates* are the *starches*. All carbohydrates, both sugars and starches, are broken down by the digestive tract and end up as glucose. The blood absorbs this glucose from the intestines and uses it for energy (fuel).

The starches—*complex carbohydrates*—are almost exclusively found in plant foods—in potatoes and beans, fruits and vegetables, grains, and in the many foods made from them, like breads, pastas, pastries and cereals.

The sugars—*simple carbohydrates*—are digested quickly, and, unless fiber is present, they enter the bloodstream as glucose within minutes. This produces a quick rise in blood sugar accompanied by an energy increase. But sugar-flooding often causes the pancreas to overreact, sending out a surge of insulin that not only brings the blood sugar back in line but sometimes drops it too low. The result may be an energy dip, often with a feeling of faintness or shakiness. The usual reaction is to grab a snack or a soda to straighten out the problem.

It works, doesn't it?

A better solution would be to eat an apple. In their natural forms nearly all carbohydrate foods contain liberal amounts of fiber. Although fiber is not generally digested by the body, it absorbs water and forms a soft mass in the intestines that acts to slow down the rate of sugar absorption.

Another solution would be to eat more complex carbohydrates, or starches. Starches are very complex molecules. Larger than sugar molecules, they take longer to digest and thus don't push up the blood sugar level as quickly. The high-fiber content of unrefined starchy foods is an additional help in leveling out the rates of digestion and absorption of nutrients.

But aren't starches more fattening than other foods?

Fat is the most fattening food. One gram of fat carries nine calories, while a gram of carbohydrate carries only four calories.

It is the refining and processing of carbohydrates that causes problems. The volume of the food goes down, while its caloric concentration goes up. That's what makes it so easy to overeat calorically when eating processed and refined foods. But when carbohydrates are eaten along with their fiber, the appetite is satisfied with fewer calories.

So what can I eat?

Potatoes and pasta, beans, barley and rice (in their unrefined form) fill people's stomachs without overloading the system with calories. Add a variety of fruits and vegetables, and it is virtually impossible to eat enough to gain weight.

Be careful, as we have mentioned, not to top off these healthy foods with butter, gravies, sauces, salad dressings, sour cream or cheese, making a nutritious, low-calorie food become a caloric disaster.

Eating complex carbohydrates "as grown," with their full complement of fiber, but without those fatty toppings, will not only allow you to eat a greater quantity of food and still lose weight, but it will also provide you with more consistent energy levels and increased endurance. This kind of eating plan will keep your arteries clean and cut your food bill in half. Where can you find a better bargain than that?

The king of the starchy vegetables is the potato. It is filling, nutritious and tasty. If you have a microwave, it only takes minutes to build a complete meal around this terrific tuber.

Are potatoes fattening?

A 5-ounce spud contains only 95 calories. The potato's reputation as a fattening food comes from the way it is served—french-fried, baked and slathered with butter or sour cream. It is the added fat, not the potato itself, that is fattening. (See chart on page 83).

Here are some tasty alternatives to high-caloric potato toppings:

- *Lentils:* Cook up a pot of lentils with onion and garlic. Ladle them onto a piping hot baked potato. Served with a green salad and whole-wheat bread, this meal will satisfy even the heartiest appetite.

- *Salsa:* Olé! It might sound a bit unusual, but salsa makes an excellent topping for a baked potato. It's available at many restaurants. Next time you eat out and the server asks, "Butter or sour cream?" say, "Neither." Ask for salsa instead.

- *Mrs. Dash Seasoning (salt-free blend):* Slice a cooked potato into wedges, sprinkle with Mrs. Dash seasoning (the one with the green cap) and bake until browned. It's the health-conscious chef's answer to french fries.

- *Mock sour cream:* Blenderize low-fat yogurt and cottage cheese, then mix in chopped chives, fresh dill, parsley, green onions or green pepper.

- *Leftover soups and stews:* There are many wonderful recipes for meatless soups and stews that can do double duty as a topping. Get creative and see what you can come up with.

CHAPTER SUMMARY

Contrary to what many believe, we need less protein and more unrefined starch in our diets. Complex carbohydrates found naturally in fruits, vegetables, potatoes, beans and grains provide clean-burning energy and increased endurance. Building your diet around these foods helps keep your arteries clean, your food bill low and your body healthy.

AN ASSIGNMENT

Add more unrefined complex carbohydrates to your diet. Enjoy whole-grain foods, beans, vegetables and potatoes. These complex carbohydrates can fill you up without weighing you down.

Chasing the Sugar High

Americans consume an average of 150 pounds of sugar and sweeteners per year for each man, woman and child. That's in excess of three-fourths of a cup a day.

I don't buy that much sugar. Where does it all come from?

Most of the sugar we consume is *hidden* sugar. Here are some of the ways sugar slips into our diets:

- *Soft drinks.* Americans average about 50 gallons of soft drinks per person per year. One 12-ounce soda may contain 12 teaspoons of sugar.

- *Desserts.* A piece of chocolate cake, for instance, may contain 15 teaspoons of sugar; a cup of frozen yogurt may have 12 teaspoons.

- *Ready-to-eat cereals.* Some, such as Shredded Wheat and Cheerios, are excellent. But look at cereals like Froot Loops, Apple Jacks and Sugar Smacks, with about 50 percent of their calories coming from sugar. These aren't cereals; they are candy!

The following chart reveals hidden sugar content:

Sugar Content		
Food	**Size Portion**	**Teaspoons of Sugar**
Soft drinks	12 oz.	8–12
Jello, puddings	1 cup	9
Jelly, jam	2 Tbsp.	8–10
Pies: apple, berry, cherry, coconut	1 slice	10
Chocolate bar	3 oz.	5
Marshmallow	10	15
Hard candy	4 oz.	20
Orange juice (unsweetened)	1 cup	6
Grape juice (commercial)	1 cup	8–10
Fruit cocktail (commercial)	1 cup	10
Chocolate chip cookies	4	6
Angel, pound cake	1 (6 oz.)	9
German chocolate cake	1 (8 oz.)	15
Chocolate milk	1 cup	8
Ice cream, sherbet	1 cup	6–8
Ice cream cone, empty	1 triple	10

Should I check labels for sugar?

Yes, but realize that sugar may also be hidden by giving it a different name. Sucrose, dextrose, lactose, fructose and maltose, for instance, are all sugars. So are corn syrup, honey and molasses.

Doesn't sugar produce quick energy?

Yes. Refined, concentrated sugars enter the bloodstream quickly. Up goes the blood sugar level, resulting in a quick energy boost—a sugar high.

But the high is only temporary because it triggers a surge of insulin. Insulin brings down blood sugar levels. In the absence of the moderating effects of fiber, insulin sometimes pulls sugar levels down too fast and too far.

A falling blood sugar often mimics symptoms of hypoglycemia, producing feelings of weakness, hunger, fatigue and letdown—the sugar blues. The usual reaction is to reach for another sugary snack, and then another, resulting in a sort of *grazing* all day long.

Instead of choosing sugary snacks, try eating an apple, a banana or a bowl of brown rice. The fiber in these foods slows down the absorption of sugar into the bloodstream. Your sugar level won't jump around so much, your energy will stabilize, and you will feel satisfied longer.

Is it true that the body can make sugar out of nearly everything we eat?

Everything but fat. For a long time people thought it didn't really matter what they ate because the body could turn it into whatever it needed. We now know that the way the body processes food, from the time it's eaten until it reaches the bloodstream, makes a great deal of difference.

The body's preferred fuel is glucose. It makes glucose from sugars and starches (carbohydrates). Although fresh fruits are high in natural sugars, they won't strain the body's blood sugar mechanism if they are eaten with their natural fiber.

Starchy foods provide another protection. Starches are broken down more slowly than sugars into the glucose the body needs. Eating starchy foods, especially *unrefined* starchy foods, along with sugar foods in their natural state helps stabilize blood sugar levels for extended periods. The ups and downs of the blood sugar curve level off, and the insulin response is activated to a lesser degree, if at all.

What are some guidelines for eating sweet foods?

Education and *moderation* are the secrets.

Proper *education* regarding food will help you avoid health problems. If you have a sweet tooth, see your dentist—well, not really. But a sweet tooth can be reeducated. For example, fruit is sweet, pleasant to the taste and full of fruit sugars. Practice satisfying your sweet cravings by reaching for a bunch of chilled or even semi-frozen grapes instead of a doughnut. Sprinkle slices of strawberries and bananas on your cereal instead of sugar. In time, your tastes will change, and you will actually prefer less concentrated sweets.

But this does not mean giving up favorite desserts altogether. *Moderation* is another guideline for eating sweet foods. Begin by decreasing the frequency of eating sugared foods. Work from daily (or several times daily) to two or three times a week. When desserts are served less often, you and your family will begin looking forward to them and enjoying them more.

Another aspect of moderation is learning to be satisfied with smaller portions. Half of a normal slice of pie or cake, eaten slowly and with pleasure, can be more satisfying than a larger piece bolted down.

Reeducate your sweet tooth. A sweet tooth can be reeducated to enjoy less concentrated sweets. Fruit and desserts sweetened with fruit are good alternatives. Try this recipe for a special treat:

Fruit Smoothie

3 or 4 soft dates	2 frozen, ripe bananas
1 cup pineapple juice	2 cups frozen fruit

Blend dates and pineapple juice until smooth. Add bananas and fruit. Blend until it is the consistency of soft ice cream. Delicious! It also makes a great topping for whole-grain waffles and pancakes.

Try these flavors:

strawberries	blueberries
peaches	crushed pineapple
orange juice	fresh blackberries

Indulge less frequently. How often do you eat desserts or sweet snacks?

__ 1–4 times/week   __ 1–2 times/day

__ 3–4 times/day   __ More than 4 times/day

If you answered more than once a day, you would benefit from reserving treats for special times.

Make the low-sugar choice. Choose low-sugar alternatives when shopping. It's not always easy to tell how much sugar a product contains because sugar can be disguised as fructose, sucrose, corn syrup and other ingredients. Whenever possible, however, buy products that you know are low in sugar.

CHAPTER SUMMARY

Sugar contains no nutrients or fiber. It is high in calories, and when eaten in excess, it can crowd more nutritious foods out of your diet.

Refined sugars and sweeteners make up about 20 percent of the calories most Americans eat—more than 40 teaspoonfuls per day. Much of this sugar is well-hidden in food and beverages. To reduce the sugar in your diet, start by substituting naturally sweet foods for sugared snacks.

If sugar has a grip on you, review these simple tips to help you reduce your dependence without eliminating sweet treats altogether. Think of some ways you can reduce the amount of sugar you are eating. List them below.

AN ASSIGNMENT

Try a fruit smoothie. Also, observe how many sweets and other sugary foods you are eating. Use the suggestions in this unit and those you listed on your own to cut back to a healthy level.

Staff of Life or Stuff of Lies?

Imitation bread—"stuff of lies," is what best-selling author Dr. David Rubin calls today's white bread. "It's a bizarre combination of the least nutritious part of the wheat grain and a number of artificial chemicals, which can be harmful."

What is wrong with white bread?

Basically, the problem with white bread is what the milling process does to wheat. A grain of wheat is made up of an outer covering (bran), an embryo (wheat germ) and the endosperm.

The bran contains most of the fiber, generous amounts of vitamins and minerals and a bit of protein.

The germ is a rich source of B and E vitamins, several minerals and fiber.

The endosperm, which makes up roughly four-fifths of the whole wheat kernel, contains protein (gluten) and starch. It is the only part used in making white flour. Ironically, the nutritious bran and wheat germ, which are removed during the milling process, are sold for animal feed.

The food industry further compounds the nutritional problems by using several artificial chemicals, such as:

- Propylene glycol (antifreeze) to keep bread white.

- Diacetyltartaric acid (an emulsifier) to save on shortening.

- Calcium sulfate (plaster of paris) to make it easier to knead large batches of dough.

Should we avoid eating white bread?

No bread is all bad. Even the white, fluffy stuff is a high-starch and low-fat food. It's just that some breads are much better than others.

Take fiber, for instance. A slice of white bread contains $\frac{1}{4}$ gram of fiber, while a slice of 100 percent whole-wheat bread contains 2 grams, and some multi-grain breads contain as much as $3\frac{1}{2}$ grams of fiber per slice. This means you'd need to eat eight or more slices of white bread to get the fiber of one slice of whole-grain bread.

Let's take a look at what wheat refining does!

% Loss of Nutrients When Refining Wheat			
Thiamine (B_1)	86%	Calcium	50%
Riboflavin (B_2)	70%	Phosphorus	78%
Niacin (B_3)	80%	Copper	75%
Iron	84%	Magnesium	72%
Pyridoxine (B_6)	60%	Manganese	71%
Folic acid	70%	Zinc	71%
Pantothenic acid	54%	Chromium	87%
Biotin	90%	Fiber	68%

What about enriched flour and enriched bread?

During the milling of wheat some twenty known minerals and vitamins are largely removed. When nutritional deficiency diseases emerged in the 1930s after the introduction of commercial milling, the industry started an enrichment program. Four of the nutrients were restored—thiamine, riboflavin, niacin and iron—and the bread and flour were called "enriched." However, in most cases, nothing has been done about the other lost nutrients.

What kind of bread is the most healthful?

Truly healthful bread contains ground-up whole grains, with the bran, wheat germ and endosperm present. Such breads have double, triple and, in some cases, quadruple nutrient value when compared with their refined counterparts.

When combined with fresh fruit, cereals, vegetables, potatoes and beans, bread makes interesting and satisfying meals and helps maintain good energy levels for long periods.

Look for the substantial-feeling loaves that aren't full of air. Look for 100 percent whole wheat, stone-ground if possible. Sprouted-wheat breads are also excellent.

Find a reliable bakery. Better yet, make your own bread.

Whole-wheat flour seems to attract weevils!

Whole-grain flours have a healthy balance of starch, protein, natural fats and fiber besides being loaded with vitamins and minerals. The bugs seem to know this. White flour, on the other hand, is such a nutritional minus that they usually won't touch it.

Store whole-grain flours in your refrigerator or freezer, or buy the grains whole and grind them up into flour just before using.

Isn't bread, even whole-wheat bread, fattening?

It isn't the bread that's fattening but what is done to it. A slice of whole-wheat bread has 70 calories—no more than an apple. If slathered with peanut butter and jam, the slice can pack close to 300 calories. As with other foods, it is not the raw materials but the overhead that can turn a low-calorie, nutritious, healthful slice of good bread into a caloric disaster.

Look past the hype. No bread is all bad, and the makers of even the least nutritious loaves capitalize on this. The wrappers boldly proclaim "Wholesome Goodness," "Natural" and "Fiber." The words and pictures are designed to make you believe you are doing your body a favor by choosing their bread.

CHAPTER SUMMARY

During the milling process, wheat loses most of its nutrients and fiber. That's why it is important to shop for 100 percent whole-wheat bread or multi-grain breads. It is better balanced and more nutritious than white bread.

An Assignment

Look for whole-grain breads when you shop. Read the labels carefully, and don't be misled by packaging that tries to pass off the "stuff of lies" as the "staff of life."

Then try these delicious alternatives for your healthy breads:

Delicious Fruit Spreads

Try these delicious toppings on whole-grain toast.

Strawberry Spread

1 cup strawberries
1 cup mashed, ripe banana

Blend ingredients in a blender until smooth. Heat to a boil in a saucepan, then simmer until the mixture thickens. Stir frequently.

Apple Butter

1 cup applesauce

Heat ingredients to a boil. Turn heat to low and simmer. Stir frequently until mixture reaches the desired thickness.

Date Butter

1 cup pitted dates, chopped fine
$\frac{1}{2}$ cup water

Boil for 6–8 minutes, stirring until smooth.

Exploding
the Myth

A sk almost any fourteen-year-old boy whether he would rather grow bigger faster or live longer, and he would probably choose the former.

Is that a relevant question?

Yes, because in the 1930s studies on laboratory animals began to turn up evidence that high-protein diets accelerated growth rate and maturation, but shortened their life span.

In animals, maybe. But everyone knows that humans need plenty of protein!

Back in 1880, a German scientist, Dr. Justus von Liebig, determined that muscles were made of protein. His protegé, Dr. Karl Voit, studying coal miners, calculated that these strong, muscular men ate around 120 grams of protein a day and announced that this was the ideal amount to eat. Getting enough protein grew to be an obsession, a myth that persists to this day.

A myth? Are you saying we don't need protein?

Modern scientific studies show that adults need at least 20–30 grams of protein a day. The human body very efficiently harvests and recycles its own protein. The only protein losses that need to be replaced are those that the body cannot retrieve, such as hair, finger and toenails and skin.

So we need only 20–30 grams of protein a day?

The National Academy of Sciences sets the RDA (Recommended Daily Allowance) for vitamins, minerals and certain foods by determining how much the body needs each day, then doubling that amount. Thus the RDA for protein has been set at 0.35 grams per pound of body weight. That works out to 60 grams for a 170-pound man and 42 grams for a 120-pound woman. Even though this is more than enough, the average Westerner continues to eat two to three times that amount!

Is that a problem?

Here are some concerns:

- Most of the protein eaten by Westerners comes from animal sources and is loaded with cholesterol and saturated fat. Because fat is well hidden, many people don't realize that meats and dairy products average from 50–85 percent of their calories as fat calories. Excess fat and cholesterol, and especially *saturated* fat, are known for their atherosclerosis-promoting effects, which lead to narrowing, hardening and increase of plaque in vital oxygen-carrying arteries. This process accelerates aging and shortens life.

- From 1850 to 2000, the average age of sexual maturity for teenage girls declined from 16.3 years to 11.9 years.

- A high-protein diet is not conducive to endurance. Athletes now load up on complex carbohydrates, not on protein.

- Excess protein places added burdens on the kidneys. Kidney disease is increasingly common in Western culture.

- High-protein diets are being associated with osteoporosis. The processing of excess protein by the kidneys requires calcium, much of which comes directly from bone stores.

Don't children need extra protein?

Yes, they do, especially during periods of rapid growth. The RDA of 0.35 grams per pound of body weight works out to be 17.5 grams of protein a day for a fifty-pound child—a little over half an ounce. Since children in Western cultures eat the same excessive high-protein diets that adults do, they are not likely to experience protein deficiencies when food supplies are adequate.

The problem may well be on the other side of the question. Accumulating evidence suggests that children eating high-fat and protein diets tend to grow bigger and to develop faster. Are they paying the price of a shortened life?

Protein Content in Food Products

U.S. Diet	Grams	Optimal Diet	Grams
3-egg ham and cheese omelet	46	Cooked cereal	9
Hashbrown potatoes	3	with milk and ½ banana	11
Toast (2) with butter, jelly	5	Toast (2) with ½ banana	4
Orange juice	1	Fruit (orange)	1
Breakfast Total	**55**	**Breakfast Total**	**25**
Big Mac	26	Pita bread (3) with	
French fries	3	tomatoes, sprouts, cucumbers	8
Milk shake	11	Three-bean salad	10
		Split pea soup with barley	12
Lunch Total	**40**	**Lunch Total**	**30**
Fried chicken (basket)	40	Spaghetti with tomato sauce	10
Mixed salad, dressing	4	Tossed salad	4
Baked potato, sour cream	8	Broccoli flowerets	5
Peas	5	Bread (2) with garbanzo spread	10
Milk	10	Baked apple with walnuts	1
Dinner Total	**67**	**Dinner Total**	**30**
Total grams of protein	**162**	**Total grams of protein**	**85**

What about the amino acid arguments?

Proteins are made of over twenty amino acids. While the body can manufacture twelve of these building blocks, eight amino acids essential for adults must be provided by the diet. People used to believe that they had to eat meat and dairy products in order to supply these "essential" amino acids. The fact that these foods are high in fat and cholesterol, lack fiber and have detrimental effects on health was, for many years, overlooked or considered irrelevant.

Now we know that these amino acids are easily available from a random selection of plant foods. This is shown in dietary patterns around the world. A staple food in Caribbean countries is black beans and rice. The amino acids missing in rice are found in the beans, and vice versa. The same is true for the corn tortillas and pinto beans of the Mexicans, and the rice and soybeans relied upon by the Chinese.

The Western world is taking a fresh look at plant foods. They are low in fat, high in fiber and free of cholesterol. And they have plenty of protein. The protein content of many vegetables exceeds 20 percent of total calories, while whole grains average about 12 percent, and most seeds and legumes contain 20–30 percent of protein.

Progressive nutritionists advise getting 10 percent of daily calories as protein. Even on a total vegetarian diet, getting this much protein is obviously no problem. In fact, when enough calories are available from a variety of *unrefined* plant foods, it is virtually impossible to create a protein deficiency unless a person suffers from a malabsorption problem.

What kind of foods come to mind when you hear the word *protein*? Beef? Eggs? Milk? Cheese? Advertisers spend millions each year making certain we feel these foods are indispensable for good health.

The fact is that animal products are not necessary in the human diet. People may choose to eat them for reasons of flavor, habit and convenience, but no one should feel that they must eat them to get enough protein or nutrients. It is time to bury the myth of high protein requirements and catch up with the times. With protein, as with much else in life, too much of a good thing is a bad thing.

Look at the Food Composition Chart on page 113. As you can see, traditional "high-protein" foods are also extremely high in fat. The Optimal Diet suggests that less than 20 percent of calories come from fat. (See page 237.) Obviously, these common protein foods fail the test.

Do plants contain protein?

Actually, all the protein you need is available from plant sources.

The following table lists a few examples:

Food Composition As Percent of Calories			
	Protein	**Fat**	**Carbohydrate**
Legumes	29	12	59
Pinto beans	26	3	71
Lentils	29	3	68
Soybeans	33	30	37
Vegetables	14	4	82
Cabbage	22	7	71
Carrots	10	4	86
Potato	11	1	88
Grains	13	8	79
Rice, brown	8	4	88
Oatmeal	14	16	70
Wheat, whole grain	16	5	79
Fruits	6	3	91
Oranges	8	4	88
Bananas	5	2	93
Peaches	6	2	93

Notice also that, unlike animal products, these sources are naturally low in fat and high in the body's preferred, clean-burning fuel, complex carbohydrates. If you eat a variety of grains, legumes and vegetables, your diet will never lack the protein your body needs for optimal performance and well-being.

CHAPTER SUMMARY

Most North Americans eat too much protein. This excess has been linked to such problems as kidney disease, gout and osteoporosis. Large quantities of meat and dairy products are not needed—vegetable sources can easily provide your body with all the protein it needs.

An Assignment

Stretch the boundaries of your diet by sampling some of the foods you have listed. Experiment with the wide variety of tastes and textures available.

CHAPTER 27

Who Needs It?

M ilk is the perfect food—for babies—mother's milk, that is. There are about 4,300 species of mammals on earth, and each mammal's milk is precisely designed and balanced for its own young. That's why cow's milk is best for baby calves.

Are you saying that cow's milk should not be given to human babies?

That's right. The American College of Pediatrics strongly urges that cow's milk should not be given to children until they are at least one year of age. Reasons? Iron absorption problems, allergies, asthma, diarrhea, ear infections, colic, eczema, nasal and bronchial congestion.

What about the rest of us? Isn't milk a healthful food?

Not really. For years we have been led to believe that milk is indispensable for sound health. However, the average Westerner eats too much fat, too much cholesterol, too much protein and not enough fiber. Milk, when calculated in percent of calories, is about 50 percent fat (much of it saturated) and 20 percent protein. It contains cholesterol and has no dietary fiber. Drinking milk puts added burdens on an already overloaded metabolic system.

How about low-fat milk? Doesn't that solve most of the problems?

Low-fat milk is an improvement over whole milk, but not as much as it seems. The 2 percent fat in low-fat milk is calculated from the weight of the milk, not from its calories. By weight, this milk is 87 percent water and 2 percent fat. By calories, low-fat milk is a 30 percent fat food.

Nonfat milk (skim milk) is the best choice for those who wish to drink milk. It has no fat and only a trace of cholesterol, yet retains its other nutrients.

How about calcium? Isn't milk famous for its calcium content?

It is true that milk is high in calcium, but before choosing to drink milk, people need to balance its calcium advantage against its problems. Here are a few to consider:

- The incidence of coronary heart disease in North America is much higher than in non-milk-drinking cultures. Whole milk, with its saturated fat and cholesterol, contributes to heart disease.

- Cultures with the highest milk consumption have the highest rates of osteoporosis, a disease rarely found in non-milk-drinking countries. Instead of protecting against osteoporosis, a high dairy consumption may actually contribute to the bone-thinning process. This happens because metabolizing excess protein can leach calcium out of the bones.

- Each animal's milk is designed to fit the growth rates of its own young. Human babies develop very slowly, and the composition of human milk reflects that difference. Animal milks may contribute to the earlier maturation noted in many of today's children.

- After weaning, humans have a high percentage of lactose intolerance (inability to properly digest milk sugar) evidenced by excessive gas, cramps and diarrhea. About 75 percent of the world's population show some degree of this problem.

- Milk is the most common cause of food allergies. More than one hundred antigens (perpetuators of allergies) may be released by the normal digestion of cow's milk. Many people with diseases such as asthma, rheumatoid arthritis and hay fever do better when they stop drinking milk.

- Most Westerners eat too much protein, and milk is a high-protein food.

- Milk is a common cause of constipation.

Many concerned people are choosing other sources of calcium such as grains, legumes, vegetable greens and, if needed, supplements.

Are you implying that adult humans don't need milk?

Many people live their whole lives in good health without drinking milk or using other dairy products. If used, milk should be consumed—preferably in nonfat form—in small quantities, such as in cooking or on breakfast cereal.

Consider this: Outside of zoos, no mammal consumes the milk of another species, and once weaned, no mammal again consumes milk. Humans are the exception. Every creature's milk is a health food only for its own offspring.

Research on nutrition has clearly demonstrated a unitary dietary principle in dealing with the Western killer diseases. There isn't one diet for treating heart disease, another for overweight and yet another for hypertension.

Instead, there is one Optimal Diet consisting of a wide variety of plant foods, freely eaten "as grown," prepared with sparing use of fats, oils, sugars and salt, and almost devoid of refined or processed foods. If animal products are eaten, they are used like a seasoning and not as the focus of the meal.

The following chart compares the typical Western diet with the Optimal Diet:

Diet Composition

Diet Constituent	U.S. Diet	Optimal Diet
Fats and oils	35–40%*	15%*
Protein	14–18%*	10–12%*
Complex carbohydrates	22%*	60–70%*
Simple carbohydrates (sugars)	20%*	minimal
Cholesterol/day	400 mg	< 50 mg
Salt/day	12–15 gm	< 5 gm
Fiber/day	10 gm	> 30 gm
Water (fluids)/day	minimal	8 glasses

* of total calories

Does milk have a role in the *Optimal Diet?*

Milk can be a part of the Optimal Diet, but it is optional. It is a concentrated protein food and should be used sparingly in nonfat form. Use it in cooking or on cereal if you desire. Soy or tofu milks make good substitutes.

CHAPTER SUMMARY

Milk is a fine food for babies, but most adults could do without the excess fat, cholesterol and protein it contains. About 50 percent of calories in whole milk come from fat. Even 2 percent low-fat milk gets 30 percent of its calories from fat. For those who wish to use milk, nonfat is preferable.

AN ASSIGNMENT

Switch to nonfat milk as you shift your eating habits toward the optimum diet. And then, why not experiment with some nondairy milk, such as soymilk or cashew milk?

CHAPTER 28

Looking for the Real Food

R*eal* food for *real* people! What an attractive thought! What an exciting promise!

Real food? What does that mean?

In the commercials, *real food* is promoted as beef, with attractive celebrities lauding its virtues. An authoritative voice explains that 3 ounces of the new, leaner cuts of beef contain no more cholesterol than 3 ounces of chicken.

What the voice didn't tell you was that lean beef, while comparable to chicken in cholesterol content, contains three to six times more dangerous, cholesterol-raising saturated fat. Besides, who eats 3-ounce portions? The average hamburger weighs close to 5 ounces, and an average-size steak weighs about 8 ounces.

But isn't meat an important source of protein?

Meat is a nutritious source of protein, but it carries along a number of problems.

For one thing, most people overestimate their protein needs. As we discussed in the protein chapter, the recommended daily allowance (RDA) for protein is a generously adequate 44–60 grams, yet most Westerners consume two to three times this much. And much of the excess is derived from animal foods.

Following World War II, for example, Americans averaged around fifty pounds of meat per person per year. Today we double that figure for beef alone. And the consumption of poultry and fish is skyrocketing. Yet we have known for years that excessive amounts of protein can be toxic to the kidneys.

An even bigger problem is the hefty doses of fat (mostly saturated) and cholesterol that a serving of meat carries. Scientific research has overwhelmingly implicated a *rich diet* as the major culprit in today's diseases. And the rich foods that are doing us in are mostly animal products, such as meat, eggs and dairy products.

The trouble is, while the human body is able to nourish itself on animal foods, it lacks the special protection against large amounts of fat and cholesterol that carnivorous animals have. In humans, excessive fat and cholesterol stack up in the bloodstream and begin attaching to the linings of blood vessels. Gradually, over time, arteries thicken and narrow, and plaque forms.

As blood supplies to vital organs diminish or are cut off, the stage is set for many of today's killer diseases, such as heart disease, hypertension, stroke, diabetes and several types of cancer.

Are you suggesting that a meatless lifestyle is better?

There are millions of people around the world getting along just fine on plant-food-centered diets. Consider some of the advantages:

Decreased risk of disease: Vegetarian populations have remarkably lower rates for many of our common diseases, such as heart disease and stroke; diabetes; arthritis; gallstones; hemorrhoids and diverticular disease; constipation; cancer of the colon, breast and prostate; osteoporosis and kidney disease.

Healthier longevity: Statistically, vegetarians are thinner, healthier and live longer than the average person.

Increased food safety:

- As soon as an animal dies, enzymes are released, which begin the process of decay. Proper preservation of meat is a continuing challenge.
- Animals ingest and store chemicals in their bodies from the fertilizers and pesticides used on their food.

- Inspectors must check carcasses rapidly, making careful examinations difficult.
- Random sampling reveals that meat frequently contains residues of growth hormones and antibiotics. Although there are laws controlling this, they are difficult to enforce.
- Today most food animals are raised on feedlots or contained in cages, with practically no exercise. The meat from these animals may contain up to twice as much fat as the meat from range-fed and free farm animals.

Environmental protection: Twenty-five gallons of water will produce one pound of wheat, whereas 2,500 gallons are needed to produce one pound of beef.

Increased world food supplies: Eighty to 90 percent of the grain grown in the U.S.A. is fed to animals. If Americans would reduce their meat consumption by 50 percent, the land, water, grain and soybeans saved would feed the entire developing world.

What has happened to natural food? Isn't that considered real food anymore?

Promoters love to extol the virtues of natural foods. Originally, the term meant foods from whole plants. Through years of careless use of the word *natural*, however, its meaning has broadened until today it is used to refer to almost anything that contains at least one healthful ingredient.

The evidence against meat and other animal products is stacking up as nutritional research confirms that a diet built around whole plant food is not only adequate, but also superior.

However, promoting health and preventing disease through diet and lifestyle do not always advance profit margins. For this reason alone, we will continue to be bombarded by expensive ads seducing us to buy products that have been given inadequate attention to health consequences.

Humans don't have the instinct to kill. We are more apt to salivate over a bunch of cold grapes than a piece of raw meat. It is comforting to know that a diet of fruit, vegetables, legumes and grains is perfectly suited to our needs—anatomically and physiologically as well as instinctively.

The wise among us will not look to the slaughterhouses for *real food*. The wise among us will find *real food* in the gardens and farms of our land. Many who have made meat and dairy products the center of their meals feel at a loss when trying to plan a meatless menu. For a while their meals seem incomplete without flesh foods.

You can satisfy your appetite on a meat-free diet. It may take awhile to adjust, but eventually this way of eating becomes acceptable and then preferable. Here is a sample menu to get you started planning delicious meat-free meals:

Sample Menu

Breakfast:

Cooked cereal (7-grain cereal) or cold cereal (Shredded Wheat, Nutrigrain) with skim milk or tofu milk and ½ of a banana or other fresh fruit sliced on top

Citrus fruit: orange or grapefruit

3 slices of whole-wheat toast with "mashed" banana topped with pineapple ring or slice of kiwi

Herbal tea

Lunch:

2 whole-wheat pita (pocket) breads stuffed with lettuce, sprouts, cucumbers, tomatoes, radishes and some low-fat cottage cheese

Split pea soup with pearl barley or rice

Fresh fruit such as papaya, pear or apple

Dinner:

Whole-wheat spaghetti and tomato sauce

Tossed salad with low-calorie Italian dressing

Slice of bread

For dessert: baked apple (microwaved)

As you are planning a more natural dietary program, build your meals around the following food categories:

Selection Suggestions

Optimal Foods

    Fruits: All fresh fruits (avocado and olives sparingly)

    Vegetables: All vegetables, greens, squash, tomatoes

    Legumes: All beans, peas, lentils, garbanzos

    Tubers: Potatoes, yams, sweet potatoes

    Grains: All whole grains, bread, pasta

    Nuts: Eat sparingly only

Optional Foods—if you insist

    Dairy: Nonfat milk, plain yogurt, skim-milk cheeses, butter-milk and low-fat cottage cheese in moderation

    Eggs: Whites only

    Flesh foods: Skinless fowl, fish fillet, lean beef—for flavor, not focus!

CHAPTER SUMMARY

The evidence keeps mounting that a diet built around whole-plant foods is superior to a meat-based diet. Meat is high in fat and cholesterol. It also lacks the fiber found in grown foods. In populations around the world, vegetarians have better health, are thinner and live longer.

AN ASSIGNMENT

After trying out the sample menu in this unit, develop your own one-day menu. Use the guidelines provided. Enjoy!

Why All the Fuss?

An insidious villain is at work in our country quietly disabling and killing more Americans each year than all the wars in this century together. *That villain is the fat in our food!*

Are you saying that eating fat can kill us?

The excess fat in food is being singled out as the most damaging component of the Western diet. That deadly duo—the high-fat, low-fiber diet—is now linked to such diverse problems as coronary artery (heart) disease, gallstones, appendicitis, cancers of the colon, breast and prostate, strokes, constipation, diverticulitis and gout, to name a few. And the list continues to grow.

Don't we need fat to be healthy?

Fat is a vital part of every living cell. Fat is also the body's back-up fuel system. We could not be optimally healthy without fat in our diets.

Problems occur because most of us eat too much fat, often in forms the body cannot easily handle. We understand that a car runs best with its specified fuel. We might get a car to run on kerosene, but it would be disastrous to its engine. Improper fuel damages the body motor also, though it is not as readily seen because a healthy body has great reserves. Up to 80 percent of the liver and kidneys can be destroyed before the organs go into failure. By the time the first angina pain or heart attack is experienced, the diameter of coronary arteries in important locations may already be reduced by 80–90 percent.

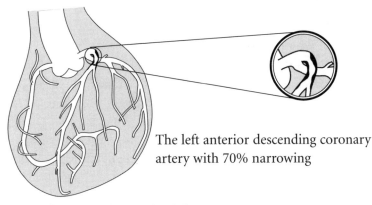

The left anterior descending coronary artery with 70% narrowing

How does fat damage the body?

An excessive amount of fat in the diet sets up conditions for the development of atherosclerosis—a hardening and narrowing of vital arteries that supply food and oxygen to the body. Excess fat makes the blood thick and sticky, slowing circulation and causing red blood cells to adhere to each other in bunches. These clumped blood cells cannot carry their full load of oxygen, and they are unable to navigate tiny capillaries. Deprived of oxygen and nutrients, body cells become susceptible to injury, disease and death.

Most high-fat foods are loaded with cholesterol, which injures the linings of arteries. The body responds by sealing off these damaged spots with extra cells. In the presence of excess fat and cholesterol, more and more Band-Aids are added, one on top of the other, until plaques are formed. When plaques grow large enough to narrow and obstruct coronary arteries, heart attacks occur. When it happens in arteries feeding the brain, a stroke takes place.

Some of the by-products of fat digestion appear to be involved in the promotion of certain cancers. These substances often cause irritation and inflammation of bowel walls, and they may be a factor in colitis and colon cancer. When adequate fiber is present, however, bowel contents move along quickly, leaving less time for toxic carcinogens to act on bowel walls.

On another front, excess fat in the bloodstream is one of the factors that depress immune cell production.

High-fat diets impair the efficiency of the body's insulin mechanism, which may lead to diabetes. The amount of saturated fat in the diet also powerfully affects blood cholesterol levels.

What can we do to protect ourselves?

It is crucial that we cut down on the fat in our diets. Butter, margarine, shortening, cooking and salad oils are nearly 100 percent fat. Meats, cheeses, eggs and whole milk average 50–80 percent of calories as fat.

Furthermore, we need a big increase in fiber intake. Fruits, vegetables, whole grains and legumes are gaining in popularity. Because these plant foods are high in fiber, low in fat and free of cholesterol, they are the ideal way to go.

The Western diet, bloated with fat, is slowly killing us. We know now that the situation can be turned around by replacing most of the fat calories we eat with unrefined plant foods.

A diet balanced in this manner will prevent many Western-type diseases and help reverse coronary heart disease and most adult diabetes. And there is more. You will enjoy better health and feel more energetic. You can also eat a higher volume of food and lose weight too!

Where Is the Fat?

Foods	% Fat Calories	Total Calories Per Cup (8 oz.)
Visible fats		
Butter, margarine, shortening, lard	98–100%	1,650–1,900
Invisible Fats		
Peanut butter	80%	1,500
Nuts	75–92%	800
Pork, beef	65–80%	500–800

Double Whopper	59%	970
Whole milk	50%	160
Ice cream	60–75%	350
Processed cheese	60–85%	450
Cream cheese	90%	850

What about the Four Food Groups?

Do you remember the *Four Food Groups* that modeled the "proper" diet issued by the U.S. Department of Agriculture in 1956? They were milk, meat, fruits and vegetables, and grain. We have discovered a lot about nutrition since then. One of the things we learned is that the emphasis on meat and dairy products made the old *Four Food Groups* high in fat, protein and cholesterol, and low in fiber. Study after study has linked this diet to increased rates of cancer, heart disease, obesity and diabetes. Clearly a big change is needed.

The New Four Food Groups

Food Group	Servings Per Day	Serving Size
Whole grains	5 or more	½ cup of hot cereal; 1 ounce dry cereal; one slice of bread
Vegetables	3 or more	One cup raw; ½ cup cooked
Legumes	2 to 3	½ cup cooked beans; 4 ounces tofu.
Fruits	3 or more	One medium piece of fruit; ½ cup cooked fruit; ½ cup fruit juice

Below are the categories from *The New Four Food Groups*. Under each heading, list foods from that category that you currently eat or would like to try. Chances are you will find that you already eat many foods from *The New Four Food Groups*.

Whole grains
  Vegetables

_____

_____

  Fruits

_____

_____

  Legumes

_____

_____

CHAPTER SUMMARY

Excess fat in foods is probably the most damaging component of the Western diet. Reducing the amount of fat we eat is essential. Butter, margarine, cooking and salad oils, meats, cheeses, eggs and whole milk—all must be limited.

AN ASSIGNMENT

Make the _New Four Food Groups_ the foundation of your diet by eating more of the foods you listed above.

Critical Countdown

W hat can turn a normal, needed, healthful substance into a dangerous killer? How can something that makes sex hormones, helps build strong bones and balances the body's stress response also choke off oxygen and damage vital organs and tissues?

Cholesterol is both hero and villain. While we cannot live without it, in excessive amounts it can kill us.

The blood cholesterol level is the single most important factor in determining a person's risk for heart disease, the nation's number one killer. A person with a blood cholesterol level of 260 mg% (6.8 mmol/L) is four times more likely to have a fatal heart attack than is a person with a cholesterol of less than 200 mg% (5.1 mmol/L).

Doesn't heredity determine cholesterol level?

Very few people have genetic cholesterol disorders. Most cholesterol levels are determined by dietary factors. Depending on what people eat, cholesterol levels can go up or down substantially within a few weeks.

How does high cholesterol cause heart attacks?

It does it by gradually plugging up the vital arteries that nourish the heart through a process called atherosclerosis.

Most heart attacks are related to plaques, which are made up mostly of cholesterol and fat. Plaques are like tire patches. They are the body's response to damaged areas in arterial walls. In response to continuing irritation over the years, the plaque slowly enlarges while endeavoring to *protect* the area. But in doing so, it also chokes off the blood flow and may eventually obstruct the artery completely.

Massive studies of world populations have documented the fact that blood cholesterol level is the most dependable predictor of arterial obstruction due to plaque formation. Research on migrant groups confirms that this is not so much a disease of genetics as it is of lifestyle. When people who have been protected by a simple diet move into a Westernized culture with its dietary excesses, their blood cholesterol levels go up, and they soon begin developing the same arterial diseases as Westerners.

But doesn't the body need cholesterol?

Yes, but we don't have to eat it. The liver manufactures all the cholesterol the body needs. Most Westerners eat an additional 400 mg of cholesterol a day. This extra cholesterol causes the trouble.

What foods contain cholesterol?

Cholesterol is found *only* in animal foods. Plant foods do not contain cholesterol. It is as simple as that.

Cholesterol Content in Foods

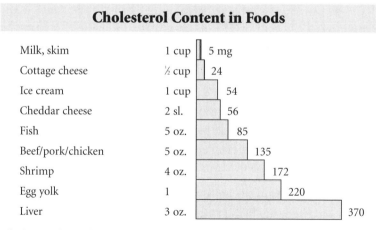

Milk, skim	1 cup	5 mg
Cottage cheese	½ cup	24
Ice cream	1 cup	54
Cheddar cheese	2 sl.	56
Fish	5 oz.	85
Beef/pork/chicken	5 oz.	135
Shrimp	4 oz.	172
Egg yolk	1	220
Liver	3 oz.	370

Cholesterol is only found in animal products.

I have heard that coconut and palm oils raise cholesterol levels.

Yes, that is true. Even though these tropical fats do not contain cholesterol, they are high in saturated fats. Saturated fats can substantially raise cholesterol levels all by themselves. They do this by stimulating the liver's cholesterol output.

Saturated fats are mostly found in animal foods like meat, eggs and dairy products, and most are solid at room temperature.

What is a safe blood cholesterol level?

Many heart researchers suggest that cholesterol levels under 160 mg% (4.1 mmol/L) will protect people from atherosclerosis.

When blood cholesterol levels are under 160 mg% (4.1 mmol/L), initial arterial damage usually heals quickly and the scars shrink. But when cholesterol levels edge past 200 mg% (5.1 mmol/L), LDL-cholesterol somehow attaches itself with greater ease to the vessel walls, causing thickening, stiffening, narrowing and plaque formation.

What are some practical ways to lower cholesterol?

It is not difficult to lower cholesterol through simple lifestyle choices. Here's how:

- *Eat less cholesterol.* Reduce the usual amount of 400 mg of cholesterol eaten to less than 50 mg a day. This means markedly reducing meat, especially organ meats and sausages, egg yolks and most dairy products.
- *Eat less fat.* Saturated fats and hydrogenated or trans-fats push the liver into overdrive in making cholesterol. These fats are twice as potent in raising blood cholesterol levels as the cholesterol we eat.
- *Eat less animal protein.* Homocysteine levels rise after a meal rich in animal protein. So does the coronary risk.
- *Eat more fiber.* Soluble fibers, plentifully found in oats, beans and fruits, bind to cholesterol and bile acids in the intestines and prevent them from being reabsorbed into the bloodstream, lowering blood cholesterol up to 10 percent
- *Medications.* Your Optimal Diet will reduce your blood cholesterol by 15–30 percent within four weeks for 90 percent

ot people. In case you are in the other 10 percent category, please check with your physician for advice about whether you need cholesterol-lowering medications.

Often there are no physical symptoms of the disease before a heart attack occurs. The best way to assess the risk of heart disease before disaster strikes is by looking at blood cholesterol levels. This is the single most important predictor of heart disease.

Do you know your blood cholesterol level? If you don't know your blood cholesterol level, don't walk, *run* to the nearest checkpoint. The procedure is simple. But more importantly, what you learn could save your life.

What is your blood cholesterol level? _____

CHAPTER SUMMARY

Blood cholesterol level is the most important factor in determining a person's risk for developing cardiovascular disease. A rich diet, one high in fat and animal products, raises cholesterol levels. Fortunately, the opposite is true also; a diet very low in fat and cholesterol, and high in fiber, has been shown to lower blood cholesterol levels as much as 15–35 percent in four weeks.

AN ASSIGNMENT

Review the five important lifestyle changes that will help you to lower your blood cholesterol.

Are Juicers the Answer?

The commercials are attractive; the live demonstrations are astounding. Piles of magnificent-looking fresh produce are fed into a little machine—and *presto*—beautiful juice!

Across the country busy people, accustomed to technological wonders and dedicated to health improvement, are welcoming yet another exciting shortcut to the good life: fruit and vegetable juicers.

Are these juicers as good as they claim?

Yes and no. Yes, they produce a nutritious drink. But no, because most do not live up to the health claims that are all too often made for them.

While juice machines deliver a product that is fairly rich in nutrients, most do so at the expense of valuable food fiber. Ten pounds of fresh produce may yield two quarts of delicious juice. But nearly all the precious *fiber* that the body so badly needs is in the five or six pounds of *pulp* that goes down the garbage disposal.

The process is reminiscent of the mills of 100 years ago that began removing bran and germ (fiber and nutrients) from grains, leaving low-fiber, nutrient-poor residues like white flour and white rice. Tragically, these foods have become the mainstay of much of the current world population.

Just what is fiber?

Fiber is the framework of plants. Because it passes through the body without being absorbed by the blood, it was long thought to be of no value. Removing it increased the caloric food density and the efficiency and speed with which it was absorbed into the bloodstream, and it prolonged the food's shelf life.

The many kinds of fiber fall into two basic groups—those that dissolve in water (soluble fiber) and those that don't (insoluble fiber).

If the blood does not assimilate it, what does fiber do?

Fiber is like a key military general to the body, controlling many different body processes.

- Insoluble fiber absorbs and holds water—from four to six times its own volume—creating soft, spongy masses in the stomach and intestines. The result? A sense of fullness occurs much sooner than with low-fiber foods, helping to protect against overeating and aiding in weight control.

- The fiber masses, acting like soaked-up sponges, fill the intestines more completely and stimulate them to lively activity. Instead of idling for several days in the gastrointestinal tract in compacted lumps, as low-fiber foods do, the spongy masses pass along much more quickly and are evacuated in twenty-four to thirty-six hours. This action cures most constipation and significantly relieves problems with hemorrhoids and diverticular disease.

- Because of the shorter transit time, there is less putrefaction (decomposition of organic material) in the intestines. There is less time for carcinogens and other harmful end-products to irritate the bowel walls. The fiber also provides insulation against damaging food residues. These fiber-related actions may explain the lower colon cancer rates among people with higher fiber intakes.

- Fiber also slows down the rate at which nutrients enter the bloodstream. This helps smooth out the ups and downs of blood sugar levels and provides more consistent energy throughout the day. A stabilized blood sugar relieves most hypoglycemia (low blood sugar) and aids in the control of diabetes (high blood sugar). Where do you find insoluble fiber? The best source is bran and whole-wheat products.

- Soluble fiber, on the other hand, helps lower blood cholesterol levels. It does this by attaching to cholesterol by-products and pulling them out of the intestines before the body can reabsorb them. Soluble fiber is especially plentiful in fruit (pectins), beans and oats.

Where do you find this seeming miracle-worker?

Fiber is abundant in all unrefined plant foods. Eating a variety of fruits, whole grains, vegetables and legumes (beans, lentils, peas) assures a plentiful supply of the many varieties of fiber the body needs.

What about meat and dairy products?

Most people are surprised to learn that animal foods do not contain any fiber. And since meat, poultry, fish, eggs and dairy products make up more than 30 percent of the calories of the typical Western diet, and much of the rest comes from sugars and other refined foods, the result is that most Westerners get only about one-third of the fiber they need each day.

What about adding wheat bran to food?

Adding wheat bran can be helpful to sedentary people on limited diets. But most people don't need fiber pills, extracted bran and other expensive supplements. It would take a whole bottle of fiber pills to supply the fiber contained in a bowl of whole-grain cereal topped with strawberries. Fiber is not something you can sprinkle on a plate of steak and eggs and make it OK.

The Western diet is extremely low in dietary fiber. First, its focus on meat and other animal products provides a shaky foundation. Any food that comes from an animal has absolutely no fiber—zero.

Second, about half of the calories in the typical American's diet are empty calories. An empty calorie provides no vitamins, no minerals and no fiber.

Chapter Summary

Fiber plays a crucial role in weight control, diabetes and digestion. It also helps protect against colon cancer. Eating a variety of unrefined foods is the best way to provide your body with the fiber it needs.

An Assignment

Start replacing fiber-free foods with fiber-filled foods in your diet. Begin with this flavorful dish:

Black Beans Over Rice

Beans

1¼ cups black beans	5 cups water
1 clove garlic, minced	1 whole onion, peeled and
½ tsp. salt	stuck with 3 whole cloves
1 cup onion, chopped	1 green pepper, chopped

Cook beans in Crock-Pot until they start to get tender. Add garlic, clove-studded onion and salt. Cook one hour more.

Sauté chopped onion and green pepper in water or broth. Take the whole onion with cloves from beans and discard. Stir in sautéed onion and green pepper.

Rice

1½ cups brown rice

Cook rice per package directions. Yields 4 cups cooked.

Salsa

16-oz. can unsalted, unpeeled tomatoes, drained
¾ cup diced red onion
1 Tbsp. lemon juice
2 cloves garlic, minced
½ cup parsley, chopped fine

In small bowl, break up tomatoes with spoon. Add other salsa ingredients. Cover and refrigerate to let flavors blend.

Serve beans over cooked rice. Top with salsa.

The Salt Assault

In our earlier discussions of health issues related to salt intake, we discovered that Americans and most other Westernized people eat up to ten to fifteen times more salt than they need. And they pay for it with high blood pressure, heart failure and other problems related to fluid retention.

Don't we need salt?

Salt contains two minerals, sodium and chloride. Sodium is the important one; every cell of your body contains sodium, as do all body fluids. We couldn't live without it. But while it is essential for body metabolism, too much sodium can cause trouble.

How does salt raise blood pressure?

Excess sodium can stay in body tissues and hold extra water. This causes swelling, which raises the blood pressure, which in turn increases stress on the heart. Every third American adult now has an elevated blood pressure. Over age sixty-five, the figures rise to 70 percent.

The average salt intake in Japan is even higher than in North America, and so is the prevalence of hypertension. Stroke, a complication of hypertension, is one of the leading causes of death in Japan.

In other societies, such as those in rural Uganda or the Amazon basin, where salt intake is very low, hypertension is virtually unknown, even in advanced age. About twenty-five years ago, Dr. Lot Page, a respected researcher, stated categorically, "Without exception, low-blood-pressure societies are low-salt societies. Conversely, mass hypertension follows mass salt consumption."

Is this true for everyone?

Not everyone is salt sensitive. Some people can eat all they want without ill effects. As many as one-half of Americans have some vulnerability to salt, however, and there is no satisfactory test for identifying them.

Salt-sensitive people retain sodium, which causes edema (swelling). Many people carry five to seven extra pounds of water weight because of excess salt in their bodies. Decreasing salt intake allows the body to shed the excess water.

It is estimated that thirty-five million Americans with mild essential hypertension could normalize their blood pressures within weeks by cutting their salt intake to 1 teaspoon (5 grams) a day.

Besides weight and blood pressure control, such a low-salt diet favorably affects PMS (premenstrual syndrome), certain headaches and some depressions. And it reduces the water logging in chronic heart failure.

What about water pills?

Water pills successfully lower blood pressure by eliminating extra water. But recent research reveals that diuretics may actually contribute to heart disease by increasing cholesterol levels 5–10 percent. Over time, these drugs may also damage the kidneys, promote gout and accelerate diabetes. Eliminating extra water by natural means is the safer way to go.

Don't people who take diuretics for high blood pressure have to take them for life?

That was yesterday's news. The word today is that up to 80 percent of those with mild essential hypertension could be eased off most blood pressure medications in response to a low-salt, low-fat diet combined with weight loss and daily walking.

But I can't stand saltless food!

Salt preferences are not inborn. *Saltiness* is a learned habit, and eating salty foods fuels the craving. Salt masks natural flavors. It takes about three weeks for your tastes to adjust to a low-salt diet. During that time food can taste pretty bland. Stick with it, however, and you will be rewarded when the delicious, natural flavors of food come out of hiding.

Can I use herbs instead of salt?

Shake the habit by seasoning with herbs and spices. After that, even so-called normal foods will begin to taste salty. (For the diehards, use salt substitutes.)

Seasoning with herbs is an important skill for the health-conscious cook to master. Here are some suggestions to spice up your meals:

1. Use no more than ¼ teaspoon of dried herbs, or ¾ teaspoon of fresh herbs, for a dish that serves four people.

2. To soups and stews that are cooked a long time, add herbs during the last hour of cooking.

3. When cooking vegetables or making sauces and gravies, cook herbs along with them.

4. To cold foods such as tomato juice, salad dressings and cottage cheese, add herbs several hours before serving. Storing these foods in the refrigerator for three to four hours deepens the flavor.

5. Remember that the correct combination of herbs and spices is the one that tastes best to you.

6. A very versatile seasoning is Mrs. Dash. Use the one without salt and low in pepper.

7. Don't overseason. Vegetables have wonderful flavors in their own right.

Remember that vegetables play a central role in the Optimal Diet. The following chart is a list of vegetables with some helpful natural seasoning suggestions:

Seasonings for Vegetables

Asparagus: lemon juice, chives, thyme, tarragon

Beans, dried: bay leaf, garlic, marjoram, onion, oregano

Beans, green: basil, dill seed, thyme, onion, tarragon

Beets: lemon juice or lemon peel

Broccoli: lemon juice, dill, oregano

Cabbage: creole cabbage with tomatoes, green pepper, garlic, onion

Carrots: parsley, mint, dillweed, lemon peel, sesame seed

Cauliflower: Italian seasonings, paprika, sesame seed

Celery: stir-fry with low-salt soy sauce, sesame seeds, tomato

Corn: bell pepper, pimiento, tomatoes, chives

Okra: try broiling for a crisp texture

Peas: fresh mushrooms, pearl onions, water chestnuts

Potatoes: parsley, chopped green pepper, onion, chives

Spinach: lemon juice, rosemary

Squash: bake with chopped apple and lemon juice

Tomatoes: sprinkle with curry powder; broil with mushrooms, green pepper and onion

What are some high-sodium foods to avoid?

Watch out for baking soda, baking powder, MSG (mono-sodium glutamate), salty snacks and anything pickled. Eat less processed foods (chocolate pudding has more sodium than potato chips), baked goods, meats, dairy products and presweetened cereals. Especially shun canned vegetables unless labeled "no salt added." One tablespoon of canned peas may contain as much sodium as five pounds of fresh peas!

How much salt is safe to eat?

Most people are genuinely amazed at how little salt the body actually needs in a day—less than 1 gram, which is about ⅕ of a teaspoon of salt a day. However, eating this small amount of salt daily would be too drastic a change for most of us. It is best to concentrate on cutting down. Instead of 10–15 grams a day, limit yourself to no more than 5 grams of salt a day. This is a reasonably safe limit for most people.

It will be necessary to become aware of where the salt is hidden, as we demonstrated earlier. The following table will give you a good idea of how easy it is to exceed the optimal level of 5,000 mg of salt a day that you need.

Salt "Bombs"		
Food/Condiment	**Amount**	**Salt (mg)**
Italian dressing	3 Tbsp.	1,900
Soy sauce	1 Tbsp.	2,300
Garlic salt	1 tsp.	4,900
Salt	1 tsp.	5,900
White bread	4 slices	2,200
Sausage	2 ounces	2,750
Cheetos puffs	4 ounces	3,700

It is obviously important to become a label reader and check the amount of sodium the food product contains. Remember, we said that to calculate the salt content, you need to multiply the sodium content by 2.5.

The average North American consumes ten pounds of salt a year. Reducing this amount to four pounds would be a major step toward better health.

CHAPTER SUMMARY

North Americans eat ten to fifteen times more salt than the body actually needs. High blood pressure, heart failure and stroke are among the sad results. By avoiding highly salted foods and reeducating ourselves to enjoy meals with little or no salt, we take a giant step toward better health.

An Assignment

Use herbs instead of salt when you cook. Experiment with new seasonings for vegetables. The switch will increase the flavor of your food and decrease your risk of high blood pressure and stroke.

Megadosing on Micronutrients

Thousands of people, attempting to become healthier, may be poisoning their bodies with large doses of vitamin and mineral supplements that can be dangerous.

I haven't studied the subject. How is one supposed to know?

That's the problem. For years we have been given *minimum* requirements and Recommended Daily Allowances (RDA) for most vitamins and a few of the minerals, but no safe *upper limits* of dosages have been established. This is because, so far, vitamins and minerals are classified under *foods* rather than *drugs,* and thus are not subjected to the extensive scrutiny and testing that drugs receive.

What kinds of damage can result from excessive intake of vitamins and minerals?

One danger is the notion that excessive doses can prevent serious diseases such as cancer, heart disease and osteoporosis. Large supplemental doses of single nutrients may interfere with the absorption of other nutrients. For example, high levels of iron appear to reduce zinc absorption, while high intakes of zinc seem to impair copper absorption.

Several vitamins are soluble only in fat. Overloads cannot be excreted, but are picked up and stored in body fat. Toxic doses of vitamin A (twenty times the RDA dose) can produce throbbing headaches, dry skin with cracked lips, joint pain and loss of hair. Pregnant women who take megadoses of vitamin A may endanger their babies.

Other fat-soluble vitamins are vitamins D, E and K. In excessive doses (three to five times the normal dose), vitamin D may become harmful to the linings of arteries, possibly encouraging plaque formation.

The water soluble vitamins (B-complex and C) were long thought to do no harm because the body could eliminate the excesses through the urine. But that rule went out the door in 1983 when mega-doses of vitamin B_6 were shown to produce disturbances in the nervous system. Excessive doses of the water-soluble vitamins have been shown to cause the body to become very wasteful of these nutrients. Megadoses of vitamin C have caused kidney stones in some people.

Another worry is that the long-term effects of megadoses are unknown. We are taking chances. Indiscriminate use can amount to over-the-counter drug abuse.

What is the safest way to get vitamins and minerals?

Ideally, we should get our micronutrients from our food. Natural foods are heavily laden with vitamins and minerals in amounts and forms that allow the body to pick and choose what it needs. Once we separate nutrients from food, in effect we concentrate certain nutrients that occur in natural balance in the food chain, running the risk of upsetting this natural balance.

What about people on limited food intake and others who pay little attention to their nutrition?

Scientists are not too concerned about people taking a daily multi-vitamin tablet that supplies the Recommended Daily Allowance for several vitamins and minerals. Supplements at reasonable levels may provide assurances in marginal situations.

But don't extra vitamins help with stress and increase energy levels?

There is no documented evidence that vitamin and mineral supple-ments make people more energetic or have any effect on stress. These micronutrients do not function in a magical manner. In excess, they will not push the pace of the body's biological reactions any more than extra gas in the tank will make a car go faster than its engine capacity allows. Energy comes from fuel foods (complex carbohydrates like grains, legumes, potatoes), not from vitamins and minerals.

While we need these micronutrients to live healthily, we need them in very minuscule amounts. People don't realize that they can put all the vitamins they need for a month into a thimble, easily.

Health doesn't come in a bottle. There is no potion or pill that can undo a lifetime of neglected health. Despite the claims of advertisers eager to make their fortune selling high-priced supplements, vitamin and mineral megadoses are not miracle cures.

People in Western countries spend billions on processed and packaged foods which have many of their nutrients removed, and then turn around and pay fantastic prices for food supplements. Wouldn't it make more sense to eat the original, vitamin-packed foods instead?

Relax and enjoy. You can't eat whole foods without getting a sizable dose of vitamins and minerals. A 6-ounce potato, for example, contains 40 percent of the Recommended Daily Allowance of vitamin C, plus fiber, niacin and potassium. It's a natural multivitamin.

All fresh fruits, whole grains and vegetables provide an abundance of nutrients. If you eat a variety of these foods every day, your need for vitamins, minerals and fiber is usually being met.

CHAPTER SUMMARY

The best place to get your vitamins is from fresh, whole foods. They're packed with the things your body needs for good health. Megadoses of vitamin supplements can be toxic. Don't upset your body's natural balance by taking too much of a good thing.

AN ASSIGNMENT

Put a permanent check mark next to broccoli on your shopping list. One cup of this leafy green vegetable, cooked, has 165 percent of the RDA for vitamin C, 50 percent for vitamin A, 20 percent for calcium, plus iron, B vitamins, potassium and other minerals.

EMOTIONAL HEALTH

Stress

Depression

Emotions

Mind Power

Beating Burnout

S tress has come to be linked with almost every medical problem we have these days—heart attacks, hypertension, heart disease, ulcers, colitis, headaches, backaches, asthma, nervous breakdowns, even cancer. Yet, too little stress can invite disease as well, causing fatigue, boredom, restlessness, dissatisfaction and depression. The challenge is to find a middle road between the two extremes.

What is stress?

Stress occurs in any situation that requires making a change. The stress involved in adjusting to some situations can produce feelings of extreme pleasure: skiing down a smooth slope, winning a race, receiving a job promotion. Other stresses may not be quite so exciting, yet cause strong feelings of satisfaction: a romantic evening, praise from a coworker, a child's good report card. Still other stresses may make us weary although they are good in themselves: a wedding or a family reunion. Then there are stresses that exhaust and depress: a job loss, legal problems, rebellious children, divorce, the death of a loved one.

Health has been called the ability to adapt to life's stresses. If so, healthy people must find ways to pace themselves by keeping their stress in positive balance.

Are stress problems getting worse?

The pace of modern life has thrown us into a kind of time warp. We are constantly urged to go *now,* see *now,* buy *now,* enjoy *now.* After all, as the ads tell us, we have only one chance in life, and we should grab all we can.

But after a few years of grabbing, getting, going, seeing and buying, we begin to feel battered and disappointed. The inevitable *pay later* comes along: burnout, debts, poor health, depression and loss of interest in life. It is a vicious cycle that has trapped many well-meaning men and women.

How can we protect ourselves from such a scenario?

It is difficult to seriously damage a healthy body with stress. You can help protect your body against the harmful effects of stress with a few simple *stress inoculations.* Some of the more important ones are:

- *Regular active exercise* for at least thirty minutes a day. Exercise produces endorphins, the *feel-good* hormones that protect the body against stress. Sunshine and fresh air also produce endorphins, so outdoor exercise is doubly beneficial.

- *A simple, plant-food-centered diet.* The body easily handles such a diet. The result is increased energy, efficiency and endurance.

- *No cigarettes, alcohol, caffeine or other harmful drugs.* These substances all chalk up substantial *pay-later* debts, often beginning the next day.

- *Adequate rest.* This includes a good night's sleep and regular times for relaxation and recreation.

- *Liberal use of water inside and out.* Drink enough water to keep the urine pale (six to eight glasses a day). A hot and cold shower each morning starts your day off right.

- *Stable life anchors.* A religious faith, a loving home, a job that makes you feel worthwhile, inspiring friends, a purpose for living—these are all vaccines against stress.

- *A positive mental attitude.* Picture a very cranky man walking to work in the pouring rain, cursing all the way. What is going on inside this man? Now picture three delighted children playing in the same rain. What is going on inside these children? Who has the most stress? The difference is not in the circumstances but in the attitude toward those circumstances.

Much of life does give us a choice. Don't procrastinate! Choose to enjoy life as it goes by. Be glad for the sunshine and the rain. Smell the flowers, return the smiles and play with children. This approach to life costs little and avoids hangovers. It exacts no *pay-later* debt. Instead, it pays generous dividends.

> For as he thinketh in his heart, so is he.
> —PROVERBS 23:7

Too much stress is a very real problem in our society. Learning to deal with it has become an important health issue since studies began linking stress to a host of physical ailments. In most cases, running away is not the answer. We must develop more positive methods of coping.

This chapter lists several ways to protect yourself against stress. List the three suggestions that seem most valuable to you.

_____

_____

_____

What can you do?

Write two or three things you can do in the near future to put each of the suggestions you listed into action. Be specific. The more clearly you imagine an action or outcome, the easier it is to achieve it.

Suggestion 1

_____

_____

Suggestion 2

_____

_____

Suggestion 3

_____

_____

Sometimes it is possible to feel emotionally stressed without knowing why. When that happens, it is helpful to make a list of the things that are bothering you. Getting the sources of your stress onto paper allows you to focus and take action. Instead of overeating, over-drinking or escaping into some time-wasting activity, you can identify the source of the problem and work toward a solution.

Stressed-out because you have too many things on your "to do" list? If so, start prioritizing your tasks. For each task on your list, ask yourself if it is something that absolutely must be done. If it is, ask yourself if it must be done right now. Cutting your list down to its essentials will help get you through those times when life seems overwhelming.

CHAPTER SUMMARY

There are many things you can do to prevent stress from taking its toll. Regular exercise, a healthful diet, and stable life anchors all play a part in combating the effects of physical and emotional pressure.

AN ASSIGNMENT

In this chapter you listed specific actions that can help you cope with the stressful world in which we live. This week, get them off the page and working for you.

Dealing With Feelings

Some experts estimate that as high as 30 percent of the adult population of developed Western countries suffer from anxiety and depression seriously enough to need help. Billions of tranquilizers and antidepressants are gulped down each year in desperate efforts to cope. Yet the problem grows.

But aren't feelings of depression a natural part of life?

Yes, depression is a normal emotion, but it can also be a symptom of a wide variety of medical and psychological illnesses.

How do people know when they've crossed the line?

Depressions are characterized by feelings of sadness and dejection, often accompanied by lessened physical activity. Let's look at some of the more common types:

- *The blues* often follow periods of excitement, fatigue or other such stresses. These depressions are short and self-limiting, rarely requiring treatment.

- *Reactive depressions* result from intense life crises such as losing a loved one or a job, a divorce, moving or a serious illness. The effect is often protective, giving time for healing to take place. Supportive measures are indicated, with more aggressive treatment if the depression is severe or prolonged.

- *Biological depressions*, on the other hand, are often inherited. They come and go, usually with no discernible cause. These depressions often respond to treatment, although they may persist for several months despite treatment.

- *Psychotic depressions* are those in which individuals lose touch with reality; they require professional care.

How can a depressed person be helped?

Diet. A simple diet of fresh, natural foods at regular intervals decreases physical stress. Eating only fresh fruit for a day or two can work wonders in clearing the mind and banishing fatigue.

Rest. Periods of quietness and calm are especially important in today's fast-paced, pressured life. As for sleep, most people do best on seven to eight hours a night.

Exercise. One of the most exciting findings of recent years has been the benefits of exercise. Regular, active, physical exercise elevates mood, increases the sense of well-being, improves sleep, relieves stress, promotes health and helps to prevent disease. A brisk one-hour walk each day will do more good for many depressed people than medication.

What else can be done for depression?

Psychological factors are important as well:

Structure. All people, whether depressed or not, need structure in their lives. Structure improves efficiency and stability.

Productivity. Humans have a basic need to do some kind of productive work, whether heading a corporation, washing a car or cooking a meal. A depressed person especially needs the feeling of completion, accomplishment and satisfaction found in doing something useful each day.

Goals. Encourage the depressed person to make a list of positive and interesting activities, and then work on one item at a time. Check each one off as it is accomplished.

Choices. Even severely depressed people can make simple, everyday choices like deciding whether to get up in the morning or stay in bed; whether to watch television all day or look for more strengthening activities; whether to dress and groom themselves or stay in a bathrobe.

Such choices, made day by day, matter a great deal because they mold the future. Even people with serious mental problems can improve their ability to cope with their life situations.

Spiritual anchors. To be worth living, life must have meaning and value; otherwise a chronic emptiness and a fluctuating sense of despair set in. Spiritual growth can bring answers to anxiety, fear, guilt and resentment. It can restore energy and zest for living.

What about medications?

Medications may be prescribed for specific reasons and for stated lengths of time. Chronic use can lead to dependency and/or increased depression.

Depression is no longer the fearful, discouraging, chronic affliction it once was. By improving physical health, developing positive mental attitudes and pursuing spiritual goals, most people can deal with their feelings of depression and live rewarding and productive lives.

This chapter presents some strategies for beating the blues. List those that might be useful to you in the spaces below:

I have the power to choose.

One of the things that sets us apart from other creatures is our ability to make choices. We do not simply respond by instinct when faced with a situation. We can think about our actions and choose between alternatives.

You have been exercising this birthright while working through the practical exercises in this book. By choosing to eat foods that prevent disease, by exercising and by your willingness to learn, you are making choices that can improve your health and energy.

Your health is not the only area where wise choices return big dividends. The decisions you make in other areas of your life are equally important for maintaining a positive outlook.

What about God?

Through the ages, millions have found comfort in time of need by turning to God through prayer to receive divine strength and wisdom.

Stories of people overcoming problems that seemed unsolvable are abundant. Even nonreligious organizations like Alcoholics Anonymous and other recovery programs recognize this and have included acceptance of the "Higher Power" concept as an important part of their programs. They recognize this Divine Power as a source of meaning, hope and inspiration that cannot be taken away by circumstance.

It is easy for the hustle and bustle of life to crowd out time for spiritual nourishment. Yet those who have endured trying times can vouch for these values. Is your spiritual life the source of inspiration, strength and renewal that it could be?

Can my family relationships help?

We humans are social creatures. We need the sense of community and belonging that comes from our relationship to others. When we feel isolated or in conflict it is much easier to slip into depression.

Think of the important relationships in your life. Imagine that each of them represents a bank account—an emotional bank account. Acts of love, kindness, understanding and respect are deposits to these accounts; acts of selfishness, impatience, anger and neglect are withdrawals.

Now think of a specific relationship. What could you do this week to add to its emotional bank account?

CHAPTER SUMMARY

Improving physical health, pursuing worthwhile goals, and developing positive mental attitudes and spiritual values can help people deal with their feelings of depression and hopelessness.

AN ASSIGNMENT

Make some deposits in the emotional bank accounts of those close to you.

Endorphins: The Happy Hormones

Feel-good drugs are almost irresistible. From cocaine to caffeine, people are reaching more and more for something that can help ease the numbing stress and paralyzing pressures that make up so much of modern life. But as evidence mounts that these drugs are destructive, scientists are discovering that a healthy body can make its own feel-good substances that are both protective and health promoting.

You mean a person's body actually makes "drugs"?

Yes. If drugs are defined as chemical substances, then the body makes thousands each day. If drugs are defined as substances used as medicine to treat disease, the answer is still yes. The human body is engaged in constant efforts to heal itself.

What kinds of "good drugs" does the body make?

The most potent man-made feel-good drugs are the narcotics. Narcotics block pain and produce feelings of extreme well-being. They are valuable in controlling severe, unavoidable pain, but over time they can become destructive and addictive.

More recently, scientists have found that the body produces narcotic-like substances of its own. These can be lumped together under the general term *endorphins*.

Want to see these hormones in action? The next time you stub your toe or smash your finger, notice how quickly the intense pain fades and a comforting numbness sets in. People injured in accidents and soldiers wounded in battle seldom realize at first how badly they are hurt. Athletes can even fracture bones in the heat of competition and not feel the pain until the game is over. These are examples of the body's endorphins at work.

Years ago, Dr. Hans Selye found that fear or anger could trigger a blast of adrenaline in the body. The extra adrenaline produced a surge of energy that enabled the person to either fight or flee the source of danger. It became known as the "fight-or-flight" response.

Research later demonstrated that feelings of fear and anger can harm the body if they are experienced over long periods of time. Other negative emotions such as grief, hatred, bitterness and resentment, if prolonged, can also exhaust emergency mechanisms and weaken the body's defenses against disease.

If negative emotions can be destructive, what about positive ones?

Norman Cousins opened the door to a new field of research when he helped heal himself of a fatal, hopeless disease by using positive emotions such as joy, laughter, love, gratitude and faith, along with sensible health practices. Since then, scientists in the field of psychoneuroimmunology have isolated many of the substances these emotions produce in the brain. They are the endorphins, and they not only block pain, but they can promote healing, strengthen the immune system, and produce wonderful feelings of well-being.

Are you saying that the way we think and feel can either damage or help heal our bodies?

Emotions are a very special part of our humanity. Clinging to persistent, negative emotions can promote disease; nurturing positive emotions benefits every part of the body. For instance, doctors are learning that they must not shut the door of hope on terminally ill patients. The caring physician who, with confidence and optimism, tells his patient, "I have a feeling you are going to be that one person in ten who conquers this disease," will often be surprised by a fulfillment of his prophecy. This is quite different from his saying, "You have only a 10 percent chance of surviving."

How else can we encourage the production of these special hormones?

We have known for a long time that physical exercise is beneficial to health. But scientists began noticing that the good feelings which came from exercise could not be explained by their fitness effect alone. Something more was happening, and that *something more* proved to be an increase in endorphins.

Could this feeling just be a result of positive thinking?

The action of both narcotics and endorphins can be reversed by a particular chemical. A person whose pain is relieved with morphine will almost immediately lose that effect if this chemical is given. A person who is feeling a heightened sense of well-being from the body's production of endorphins will also lose that effect if this chemical is given. It is that specific.

But, yes, endorphin production is a result of positive thinking. Solving conflicts, banishing hatred and resentment, cultivating a loving, generous, thankful disposition, finding a strong faith—all these will boost the production of endorphins in our brains and strengthen the ability of the body to resist disease. And the physical benefit of a daily walk is the frosting on the cake.

Happiness Quiz

Part 1

It is easier to be happy when you feel healthy. Which of the following are you doing to physically boost your state of mind?

☐ Exercise daily (preferably in the fresh air). Studies show that exercise is one of the most effective cures for the blues. Certainly, it is the least expensive.

☐ Avoid caffeine. Too much caffeine shortens your fuse and decreases your tolerance to life's stresses. It can also cause insomnia, robbing your body of much-needed rest.

☐ Avoid alcohol. Alcohol is a depressant, yet many people turn to it during periods when they are experiencing negative emotions. That is a little like throwing gasoline on a fire. You don't need a depressant when you are feeling down.

☐ Eat a low-fat diet. Build it around whole grains, vegetables and fruits. On this diet you will feel better, look better and have more energy. All of these benefits create an environment where positive emotions can flourish.

☐ Get enough fresh air. A well-ventilated house and frequent deep breathing helps keep your blood oxygenated. This is essential for being mentally and emotionally in top form. Fresh supplies of oxygen help keep you awake and alert.

Part 2

The mind and body are linked. Just as it is difficult to be happy when you are feeling the effects of physical illness, it is also hard to feel healthy when you are in conflict with yourself or others.

The following habits cultivate a happy, thankful attitude. How many of them are you developing?

☐ Count your blessings. Every one of us has much to be thankful for.

☐ Work toward harmony in relationships. If you nurture the negative emotions of bitterness, envy and jealousy toward others, you rob yourself of much joy. On the other hand, developing a forgiving, caring attitude brings happiness and friendship into your life.

☐ Work for the good of others. Reaching out beyond yourself to touch others helps you as much as it does those whose lives you brighten.

☐ Take time for spiritual renewal. The great men and women of all times have drawn strength and inspiration from their faith in Someone greater than themselves. This faith has helped them overcome obstacles and achieve greatness.

CHAPTER SUMMARY

The body makes its own feel-good substances—endorphins—that are both protective and health promoting. Physical exercise and a positive mental attitude boost the production of these endorphins in the brain and increase the body's ability to fight disease.

An Assignment

Look back over the *Happiness Quiz.* Are there things that you aren't doing that might give your emotional life a boost? Choose one item and focus on it this week.

You Are What You Think

Aristotle once said that a healthy body and a healthy mind were somehow intertwined, but the idea has traveled a rocky road ever since.

I thought that idea was pretty well accepted these days!

Yes, and no.

Some scientists still question a direct link between emotion and disease because they are not able to prove conclusively that a person's state of mind is able to cause or cure a specific disease.

What is emerging, however, is a better understanding of the body's immune system. While scientists can't take one particular emotion, such as anger, and relate it to a specific disease like a heart attack, they can now measure the body's immune response to specific stresses.

What is the immune system?

The human body is protected by millions of *fighting units*, circulating in the blood stream. These consist of different types of *soldiers,* each group having its own specific function. *Central Control* can order out new *units* when disease invades the body. During times of peace the numbers are reduced and the *fighters* become patrols. This is a simplified explanation of the immune system.

What affects the immune system?

A healthful diet, physical fitness and positive emotional states can stimulate and strengthen the body's immune system. On the other hand, illness, drugs and excessive stress can weaken it. For example, AIDS occurs when the entire immune system has been decimated.

Emotions can affect it?

Very likely. Scientists report that people in depressed and negative emotional states may be especially vulnerable to diseases affecting the immune system, such as asthma, rheumatoid arthritis and cancer.

How can feelings affect health?

Scientists call it the *placebo effect.* Perhaps the best way to explain it would be to illustrate it with a story.

Working late one night, I was nearly overcome by sleepiness.

Remembering that my secretary keeps a jar of instant coffee in her desk, I added several tablespoons of the powder to a cup of water, gulped it down and waited.

Within ten minutes I felt energized—yes, caffeine mobilizes blood sugar. Then came heightened alertness—yes, it also stimulates the nervous system. I rushed to the bathroom, confirming that caffeine is also a diuretic. The boost lasted the three hours I needed to finish the project.

Next morning I confessed to my secretary. She listened and began to smile.

"I'm glad my coffee helped," she said. "But didn't you notice it was *decaffeinated?*"

It worked because you thought it would work.

Yes. This *placebo effect* is commonly used to test new medicines. One group of test subjects is given the real thing, while another group receives a look-alike. Surprisingly, placebo subjects often report as good, and sometimes even better, results than those who receive the actual medication.

In short, thoughts and emotions directly influence the mind, which in turn powerfully affects the body. Reports are on record of people who believed they were going to die, and they did, though no direct cause for death could be found.

Will positive emotions, then, strengthen the immune system?

Newer studies are suggesting that a stable emotional life is as important to good health as more traditional influences such as improved diet, regular exercise and the avoidance of alcohol, tobacco and other drugs.

Positive emotions and sensible health practices, it appears, can stimulate the production of endorphins. These mysterious substances are manufactured by the brain and can produce remarkable feelings of well-being. Apparently they *pep up* the immune system as well. Endorphins, in other words, help make you feel better while they also help make you well.

So I can cure myself by thinking nice thoughts?

You should never neglect whatever *physical* cures exist for a health problem. Giving up smoking, watching your weight, getting regular exercise, taking medication—none of what I have said makes these things unimportant.

But in addition, keep an eye on your attitude. As King Solomon said:

> A cheerful heart is good medicine, but a crushed spirit dries up the bones.
> —PROVERBS 17:22, NIV

And Paul adds:

> Whatever is true, whatever is noble, whatever is right, whatever is pure, whatever is lovely, whatever is admirable—if anything is excellent or praiseworthy—think about such things.
> —PHILIPPIANS 4:8, NIV

How can I use my mind and emotions to work for me?

We have seen that the mind and emotions have a powerful influence in our physical lives. But how do we harness that power to work for us? One answer is through the power of questions. Questions have a unique power—a power to focus. A question is like a lens, turning the focus of your attention toward a specific problem or situation. When you ask yourself a question, your mind automatically goes to work looking for an answer.

The right questions can affect all areas of your life—from your relationships, to your attitudes, to your creativity and ability to solve problems.

Here are five questions that only you can answer. If you back your answers up with action, each of them can have a tremendous effect on your life. Be specific, and ask yourself the following:

1. What is the one thing I could do that would have the greatest positive, long-term effect on my life?

   _____

   _____

2. What is one thing I could do that would improve my relationship with someone I care about?

   _____

   _____

3. What is there in my life, right now, that is worth being happy about? (Ask this one often.)

   _____

   _____

4. What can I do today to develop a more healthful lifestyle?

   _____

   _____

5. If it were someone else in my situation, what would I tell them to do? (Ask this question when you are in a bind.)

   _____

   _____

Don't ask yourself negative questions like *Why am I so dumb?* or *Why can't I stick to an exercise program?* Those questions focus your mind in a negative direction. Instead, rephrase them in a positive, productive way:

What can I do in the future to avoid this mistake? Or, *How can I adjust my schedule to make exercising easier?*

CHAPTER SUMMARY

Thoughts and emotions directly influence the mind, which in turn affects the body. Research suggests that a stable emotional life is as important to good health as more traditional factors such as exercise and diet.

AN ASSIGNMENT

Use the five questions listed in this chapter and try to come up with several more of your own. You will be surprised at the power of this simple technique.

NATURAL REMEDIES

The Ultimate Diet

Vegetarians are sprouting up all over—more than 16 million people in the United States alone do not eat meat anymore. Once stereotyped as food fanatics or left-over hippies, vegetarians are now widely respected. They are considered healthier and their diet more ecologically sound.

Why go to the trouble of being a vegetarian?

Seven out of ten Americans suffer and die prematurely of three killer diseases: heart disease, cancer and stroke. In his comprehensive report to the nation titled *Nutrition and Health,* C. Everett Koop, MD stated unequivocally that the Western diet was the major contributor to these diseases. He confirmed that saturated fat and cholesterol, eaten in disproportionate amounts, were the main culprits. He reminded people that animal products are the largest source of saturated fat as well as the only source of cholesterol. To compound the problem, Dr. Koop pointed out, these foods are usually eaten at the expense of foods rich in complex carbohydrates such as grains, fruits and vegetables.

The average risk of heart disease for a man eating meat, eggs and dairy products is 50 percent. The risk for a man who eliminates meat from his diet is 15 percent. However, the coronary risk of a total vegetarian who eliminates meat, eggs and dairy products drops to 4 percent.

An editorial in the *Journal of the American Medical Association* commented on these advantages, stating that a total vegetarian diet can prevent up to 90 percent of our strokes and 97 percent of our heart attacks.

Going beyond prevention, Dr. Dean Ornish published studies proving, beyond a shadow of a doubt, that a very low-fat vegetarian diet could reverse heart disease in coronary patients.

The risk for cancer of the prostate, breast and colon is three to four times higher for people who consume meat, eggs and dairy products on a daily basis when compared to those who eat them sparingly or not at all. In addition, vegetarian women have stronger bones and fewer fractures, and they lose less bone as they age.

Studies of long-lived vegetarian people like the Hunzas, who are healthy and active into advanced age, contrast sharply with the short lifespans and increased disease rates of Alaskan Eskimos, who depend largely on the meat they catch from the sea.

Are vegetarians able to meet their nutrient needs?

Easily. The RDA for protein is 44–60 grams for adults, which works out to around 10 percent of calories eaten. A beefsteak offers about 25 percent of its calories as usable protein. The protein content of most fresh vegetables averages around 20 percent of total calories, and grains usually exceed 10 percent. In addition, dried beans and peas carry close to 25 percent of calories as usable protein. So there is plenty of protein in plant foods, which are also low in fat, high in fiber and contain no cholesterol.

Studies show that complementary proteins and iron supplies are essentially not problems in humans eating a variety of plant foods, although *pure* vegetarians may require small supplements of vitamin B_{12}.

Will switching to a vegetarian diet affect my weight?

If you replace the meat in your diet with doughnuts, Twinkies, french fries and other high-fat, high-sugar morsels, then, yes, you will probably gain weight.

However, if you choose to eat more foods as grown, simply prepared without adding those nutrition-depleted calories, you can shed excess weight and stabilize at a healthier level.

What would be the ecological effects?

Shifting toward a vegetarian lifestyle would greatly ease the environmental impact of our present meat-centered diet. Pollution from animal-based agriculture is greater than from all other human and industrial activities combined. Overgrazing and intense cultivation of land for production of animal foods contribute substantially to the massive erosion and the irretrievable loss of six billion tons of valuable topsoil annually in America.

But the impact of a meat-centered diet goes beyond North America. In Central America, for example, irreparable damage with global implications continues on a daily basis. Americans eat over 200 million pounds of Central American beef every year. Powerful landowners have destroyed more than 25 percent of the region's rain forests, turning them into grazing lands for the cattle needed to supply the ever-expanding hamburger chains. About fifty-five square feet of land is needed to produce one quarter-pound hamburger.

Doesn't this affect the world's food supplies?

By moving toward vegetarianism we could use our grains and beans to feed the world's hungry people instead of the world's cattle and poultry. The amount of land needed to feed one person consuming a meat-based diet would feed twenty vegetarians. One acre of land yields 165 pounds of beef but 20,000 pounds of potatoes. To produce one pound of edible flesh from a feedlot steer requires 10 pounds of grain and soybeans. It's a poor conversion system that operates at a 10 percent efficiency level!

The evidence against meat continues to grow as it once did for cigarettes. The vegetarian diet is proving to be the ultimate diet—maximizing health, preventing disease, releasing food to the hungry and preserving the planet. It's time for Americans to stop slaughtering nine million creatures every day for food.

OK, I'm convinced. How do I make the transition?

Some people can switch to a vegetarian diet *cold turkey,* but others do it more gradually, eliminating red meat first, then poultry, fish and finally, dairy products.

Another idea is to begin with one or more meatless days a week. As you experiment with vegetarian dishes, you can gradually increase the number of meatless meals.

Switching to a less meat-dependent diet is really not such a big deal. We already eat bean burritos, pasta and other standard meatless fare. Stretch your imagination, enjoy the varied tastes, save on your food dollar and savor a new level of health.

What about a quick lunch?

For busy people, lunch is often a difficult meal. The temptation is to grab something quick. Fortunately, *quick* does not have to mean a burger from a fast-food restaurant. With some advance planning, you can take a healthful lunch wherever you go. Here are tips for taking the Optimal Diet on the road.

- *Bring a thermos:* A thermos lets you carry along delicious soups and stews. Who said lunch had to be built around a sandwich?

- *Use resealable plastic containers:* Tupperware-type containers are excellent for raw, cut vegetables, salads and leftovers. Be creative!

- *Microwave it:* If you have access to a microwave, bring a potato and some type of topping for lunch. It takes just minutes for a nutritious, piping hot meal. Who knows? Your example could inspire a lunchtime trend toward good eating.

CHAPTER SUMMARY

Vegetarians are no longer viewed as food fanatics and countercultural oddballs. Studies confirm that most live longer, healthier lives, and that their diets are more ecologically sound. Making the transition to a meat-free diet can be a challenging adventure, leading to a new level of good health and well-being.

AN ASSIGNMENT

Meat can be hazardous to your health. Start eliminating it from your diet by making your own delicious lunches.

What Follows
the Swallows

Proteins, fats and carbohydrates are the major constituents of food. They carry the food's energy to the body. The body digests each in an orderly fashion, yet at different rates. It digests simple carbohydrates (sugars) quickly, while fats take longer. Proteins and complex carbohydrates (starches) fall somewhere in between.

Is there some benefit in eating a starch food, for instance, at one meal, and a protein food at a different time?

Nature doesn't support this idea. All plant foods and some animal foods are combinations of carbohydrate, protein and fat. Broccoli and peas, for example, contain a fair percentage of protein, and even lettuce has a little fat.

To get a pure carbohydrate meal you would need to eat white sugar or the starchy residue that is left after removing the gluten from white flour. A pure protein meal could be egg whites or dry cottage cheese curds. For the fat meal a few tablespoons of butter or cooking oil would do. *Pure foods,* in this sense, don't occur in nature, though they can be manufactured.

How does the stomach handle these different food constituents?

Digestion is the process by which the body breaks food down into its component parts so that the sugars and starches of the carbohydrates become glucose, fats become fatty acids, and proteins become amino acids. The blood can pick up these substances from the intestines.

Only a part of digestion occurs in the stomach. The rest occurs in the mouth and intestines. In an amazingly orderly fashion, carbohydrate digestion begins in the mouth with the saliva and continues in the stomach. Protein digestion begins in the stomach and continues in the intestines. Fat is digested entirely in the intestines.

Does the acidity or alkalinity of foods affect this process?

The stomach has three basic functions:

- It breaks food particles down to a more uniform size by muscular action.

- It brings the food mass to the needed consistency by adding or absorbing fluid.

- It brings the stomach contents to the necessary degree of acidity by secreting acidic digestive juices. This phase accomplishes those parts of digestion that require an acid medium.

When the stomach contents go on to the intestines, they become alkalinized by juices that the pancreas secretes. The digestive process is completed in the intestines.

Do some foods bog down this process?

Foods high in fats are the worst offenders. The body cannot digest fats until they are alkalinized and emulsified by the intestinal juices (much as the grease on your hands cannot be removed until it is emulsified with soap and hot water). But the body has protective mechanisms that meter the fat from the stomach to the intestines so that the emulsification process isn't overwhelmed. If the amount of fat in a meal is not large, it will make little difference in digestion time. But a meal high in fat takes considerably longer to pass through the stomach.

Is there an ideal balance of foods?

The body can handle three or four kinds of whole plant foods with maximum efficiency and minimum stress. A more complex meal takes longer to digest and exacts a higher energy price from the body.

Eating snacks between meals disrupts the orderly digestive processes and stresses the stomach. Digestive problems will be slight if the stomach is presented with a simple meal, allowed to digest it and then is given time to rest awhile before adding more food. Ideally, meals should be four or five hours apart.

How can I get relief?

How do you spell relief? If you are like most North Americans, you spell it D-O-L-L-A-R-S. Each year we spend millions on pills and potions to quiet our angry stomachs. There is a better way, of course—stop overloading your stomach and give it the rest it needs.

Before reading on, answer this question as accurately as you can: "How often does your stomach protest?"

___ Never
___ Several times a year
___ Several times a month
___ Weekly
___ Every day

If you frequently have indigestion or an upset stomach, and your doctor has ruled out more serious problems, it may be your eating habits that are causing you grief.

Answer the following questions with a *yes* or *no*:

1. ___ Do you have regular eating times?

   Your body thrives on a regular schedule, not only of eating, but of waking, sleeping and exercise.

2 ___ Do you often eat between meals?

   Review the discussion above regarding the effects of snacking.

3. ___ Are your meals spaced four to five hours apart?

   Spacing meals several hours apart allows the stomach to work at its own pace. Food from one meal is completely digested before the next one arrives.

4. ___ Do you drink coffee?

Coffee, even decaffeinated, contains substances that can irritate the lining of the stomach. Too much of this substance can send your stomach into rebellion.

5. ___ Do you eat right before going to bed?

The stomach, like the rest of your body, needs rest. A meal or snack late in the evening forces it to work overtime.

What about gas?

Many people adjusting to a high-fiber diet experience problems with intestinal gas. This is especially true when legumes are on the menu. Here are some suggestions that can help:

- For occasional intestinal gas, try some pharmaceutical-grade charcoal. It absorbs gas and provides a measure of relief. It is available as powder, tablets, syrup or capsules and is sold over the counter.

- To reduce gas caused by cooked dried beans, try soaking them overnight, then discarding the water and replacing it with fresh water for cooking.

CHAPTER SUMMARY

Digestion is a marvelous process. To help your body work with maximum efficiency, space meals four to five hours apart and avoid snacking.

AN ASSIGNMENT

Give your stomach a break by spacing meals further apart. Not interrupting the digestive cycle with snacks will sweeten the disposition of a cranky stomach.

The Rise and Fall of Oat Bran

Once billed as a quick fix for pulling down stubborn cholesterol levels, oat bran cut a blazing swath across public awareness. Foodmakers jumped to take advantage of the windfall, deciding that nearly everything went better with oat bran. An oatmeal war broke out. Oat bran became scarce, and the price shot up.

Was there scientific evidence for the claims?

Allowing for the usual exaggerations, oat bran did appear to be remarkably effective. In one study, for instance, men with high blood cholesterol levels were given a bowl of oat bran cereal and five oat bran muffins each day along with their usual food. Another group, with similar cholesterol levels, ate their usual diet. After ten days the oat bran group had dropped their cholesterol levels by 13 percent.

What was the secret?

The secret appeared to be in oat bran fiber. There are many kinds of fiber, but they all fall into two basic groups: those that dissolve in water (soluble fiber), and those that don't (insoluble fiber).

Insoluble fiber absorbs water in the intestinal tract, increases stool bulk and helps speed the movement of food through the intestines. It has a valuable laxative effect and helps to stabilize blood sugar.

Soluble fiber, on the other hand, is the type that affects cholesterol. Cholesterol is a by-product of digestion. Without soluble fiber to help carry it out of the intestines, most of this cholesterol would be reabsorbed into the bloodstream, adding to the already high levels found in most Westerners. It was believed that oat bran fiber had an exceptionally high affinity for these cholesterol by-products.

Sounds good. Was there a problem with that?

The prestigious *New England Journal of Medicine* published a study several months later that appeared to pull the rug out from under the hype. The mighty oat, it suddenly seemed, was not what it was cracked up to be. Besides, people were getting tired of oat bran mush. Even the muffins were becoming a bore.

So it was just another fad!

Not altogether. The new study didn't debunk oat bran as a food. Instead, it demonstrated that oat bran didn't act in the way people presumed it did. It was not a *magical potion* that could be gulped down to ream out the blood vessels or sprinkled on harmful foods to make them OK.

What the study showed was that a big bowl of any hot starchy cereal, eaten for breakfast, would displace an appreciable amount of bacon, eggs, sausage croissants and other foods that kick in the liver's cholesterol-producing machinery.

And other studies demonstrated that, while eating soluble fiber might lower cholesterol levels, oatbran fiber held no advantage over the soluble fibers in other foods, such as beans and fruit.

These observations make sense. Any dietary change where low-fat, starchy, no-cholesterol plant foods replace high-fat, high-cholesterol animal foods has been repeatedly shown to be effective in lowering cholesterol levels.

You're confusing me!

People who eat lots of plant foods will get all the fiber they need, both soluble and insoluble. However, for people unable or unwilling to follow such a diet, adding oat and other types of bran to their food is a helpful step.

The moral of all this? It is folly to focus excessively on a single food or nutrient. While sensationalized discoveries and simplistic solutions to complex health problems are the darlings of the media and the advertisers, the oat debacle should enlarge our understanding of the role that the wide variety of available plant foods play in promoting health. Grains in almost any form make for healthful eating. But to eat largely of a single extract, such as oat bran, produces a lopsided diet.

Studies over the years have demonstrated that a high-fiber, low-fat, meatless diet will lower cholesterol levels 20–35 percent in four to eight weeks for most people. Adding oat bran to such a diet contributes little.

Why the hype then?

Oat bran is an example of what can happen when the media or food companies blow a study out of proportion. Often they do it without regard for the significance or reliability of the findings. Oats and oat bran are nutritious, health-promoting foods. They should be part of a well-balanced diet. But preoccupation with exciting new discoveries and the eternal desire for the quick fix continue to encourage extreme and impractical solutions to real health problems.

A balanced, healthful lifestyle may not grab headlines or create profitable new markets, but it brings improved health that lasts.

What about bread packaging?

Another example of "partial truth" selling products relates to bread packaging. Food companies are experts at manipulating the truth. They don't necessarily lie, but they often do slant the truth in their favor by publicizing only that which supports their purposes.

Imagine that you design packaging for a large bread company. Your instructions are to create a new wrapper for the company's loaves of white bread. When shoppers see the wrapper, you want them to choose your bread over that of the competition. What kinds of things could you put on the wrapper to convince people to buy your bread?

Your market research shows that consumers associate the words *whole wheat* with good nutrition. The bread you are selling isn't made from whole-wheat flour, but your research also shows that many customers think the words *whole wheat* and *100 percent wheat* mean the same thing. They don't. *Whole wheat* means the flour used came from the whole-wheat grain, while *100 percent wheat* means only that the flour used came from wheat entirely rather than some other grain.

You put the words *100 percent wheat bread* in large letters on the wrapper, and it works. More customers buy your loaf of bread, feeling confident that they are choosing a nutritious loaf. You win, but at your customer's expense.

How do I decide?

With so many people slanting the health news for their own purposes, how do we know what to believe? Good common sense is one answer. When you read about the results of a study or hear the claims of an advertiser, ask yourself the following questions:

Believability Checklist

1. Who is making this claim? Be suspicious if it is the producer of the product.

2. What do they have to gain by publicizing this information? What is their motive?

3. Do other studies agree with these claims, or is this an exception or "new" finding being picked up by the media? The news media love a sensational story. As a result, they often publish the results of flawed or biased studies.

4. Does the claim sound like magic? If it sounds too good to be true, chances are it is.

5. Is a drug or food touted as the answer to reversing a chronic condition brought on by long-term lifestyle patterns? Beware of the promise of a *quick fix*.

6. Does the claim contradict the principles of balance and common sense?

Chapter Summary

Preoccupation with new discoveries and quick fixes focuses attention away from the need for a healthy lifestyle and well-balanced diet. There is no single food that will cure a lifetime of poor health choices. Only by adopting a balanced lifestyle can one begin to enjoy the many benefits of good health.

An Assignment

Look at health news with a critical eye. Use the *Believability Checklist* to screen out misinformation.

Jump-Start Your Day

M any people cannot face food when they crawl out of bed. A quick cup of coffee is a standard adult breakfast for many. An increasing number of children arrive at school having eaten nothing at all.

Why bother with breakfast?

A group of scientists spent ten years studying the effects of different kinds of breakfasts vs. no breakfast at all on people of different ages.

A good breakfast, they concluded, can help both children and adults be less irritable, more efficient and more energetic.

More recent studies have even linked healthy breakfasts with less chronic disease, increased longevity and better health.

A *good breakfast,* by the way, is one that provides at least one-third of the day's calories. Start your day with a whole-grain cereal, whole-grain bread and a couple of whole, fresh fruits, and you'll find that your energy level stays high throughout the morning.

What's wrong with orange juice and a Danish?

You need something with more fiber in it. Although fiber isn't digested by the body, it does absorb water as it moves through the stomach and intestines. The resulting spongy mass acts as a gentle barrier to the food particles suspended in it so that they are not absorbed too quickly.

On the other hand, fiberless foods, especially sugared foods and drinks, quickly pass into the bloodstream and cause blood sugar levels to rapidly rise and fall. That helps explain why your energy and efficiency drop off in the later morning hours when little or no fiber-containing foods are eaten at breakfast.

But I'm not hungry until mid-morning!

Probably the biggest reason people feel that way is that they eat a large meal in the evening. (TV snacks don't help either!) When they go to bed, their stomachs are still busy digesting all that food. But the stomach needs rest, too. An exhausted stomach does not feel like taking on a big breakfast.

The solution?

- Eat a light supper at least four hours before bedtime, or even skip supper a few times.

- Eat or drink nothing but water or fruit between supper and bedtime.

If you do these two things, you'll be ready to *break the fast* with breakfast after the long night of resting the stomach.

Won't skipping breakfast help me lose weight?

Surprisingly, no. The Iowa Breakfast Studies demonstrated that the omission of breakfast does not have an advantage in weight reduction. It is actually a disadvantage because those who omit breakfast accentuate their hunger and eat more snacks and food the rest of the day to make up for the lack. They also suffer a significant loss of efficiency in the late morning hours.

But I don't have time to eat breakfast.

Many people are in the habit of staying up late, then sleeping in as long as they can in the morning. Although a few people work more efficiently at night, most don't fit that timetable.

Try going to bed early enough so you can wake up in the morning feeling refreshed and with time to spare. Begin the day by drinking a glass or two of water to rinse and freshen your stomach. Pull on your gym clothes and get some active exercise, like a brisk walk. Shower and dress for the day. Then fix and eat a hot breakfast.

This works with children, too. Put them to bed early enough so that they wake up in time to join the family around the breakfast table.

A good breakfast boosts your energy, increases your attention span and heightens your sense of well-being. You'll be less apt to cheat on your diet by snacking. And you'll be in better control of your emotions.

What a great way to start your day!

Breakfast Choices				
	Calories	**Fat (gm)**	**Salt (mg)**	**Chol. (mg)**
"The American Way"				
Bacon (3 sl.)	129	12	574	60
Scrambled eggs (3)	330	24	1,230	675
Hashbrowns (1 cup)	355	18	3,265	0
Danish roll (1)	274	15	595	35
Hot cocoa (1 cup)	213	9	295	25
Orange juice (1 cup)	120	0	6	0
"The Better Way"				
7 Grain cereal (1 cup)	159	1	400	0
Banana (1)	95	0	3	0
Nonfat milk (1 cup)	88	0	318	0
Grapefruit (½)	66	0	5	0
Tofu (1 cup)	118	7	1,233	0
Hashbrowns, no oil (1 cup)	101	0	22	0
Whole-wheat bread (1 sl.)	61	1	330	0

Will this make the most of my day?

As discussed, many studies have emphasized the importance of breakfast. If you want to make the most of your day, fuel your body with the right stuff. The following quiz will help you examine your morning eating habits. Answer *yes* or *no* as accurately as possible.

The Breakfast Quiz

___ 1. Do you skip breakfast often? Mom was right—breakfast really is the most important meal of the day. If you skip it, you are starting the day at a disadvantage.

___ 2. Do you get up in time to eat a good breakfast? If not, how could you change your routine to give yourself time for a nutritious morning meal?

___ 3. Are you hungry in the morning, or is your appetite a late riser? Review the two solutions to this problem discussed in this chapter. What are they?

_____

_____

___ 4. Is your usual breakfast high in fiber from whole fruits and grains? The fiber and complex carbohydrates in whole foods provides a steady release of energy that most processed breakfast foods lack. It will keep you going strong all morning.

___ 5. Is your breakfast high in fats and cholesterol? A traditional breakfast of eggs and sausage can be the most deadly meal of the day. Breakfast meats are loaded with fats, cholesterol and salt. Eggs can send your cholesterol skyrocketing. The sausage and egg breakfast needs to go the way of the dinosaur if you want to avoid extinction.

How well have you been eating?

What did you have for breakfast this morning? List everything you ate.

_____

_____

Based on what you have learned, how can you improve the quality of your breakfasts?

_____

_____

CHAPTER SUMMARY

A good breakfast boosts your energy, increases your attention span and heightens your sense of well-being. Recent studies have even linked healthy breakfasts with less chronic disease, increased longevity and better health.

AN ASSIGNMENT

Make eating a good breakfast a priority. Note any changes in your energy level and productivity. The recipe below will help get you started.

Cashew Oat Waffles

Blenderize the following ingredients until smooth. Bake in a preheated waffle iron for 10–12 minutes:

2 cups water	1½ cups regular rolled oats
⅓ cup raw cashews	½ tsp. salt (optional)

Top with mashed bananas, fresh or frozen berries, apple sauce or crushed pineapple.

Today's Fountain of Youth

The fabled "fountain of youth" lured ancient adventurers into a lifetime of fruitless searching. In time, it became a symbol for an impossible dream. That was yesterday. Today, science seems able to put at least part of this dream within reach of nearly all of us.

What do you mean?

When the explorers were searching for a secret spring that would maintain perpetual youth, many people were dying in early adulthood of infectious diseases. Today, improved sanitation and hygiene, along with antibiotics, have almost eliminated those diseases. The battle has now shifted to degenerative diseases. These are the maladies that are now robbing us of our energy, disabling us prematurely and killing us s-l-o-w-l-y.

The good news is that greater vitality, better health and longer life can be ours through regular, brisk physical activity.

Do you mean *EXERCISE?* Can it really do all that?

Take a look at the facts. The adage *"Use it or lose it"* applies not only to muscles and bones but also to heart, lungs, brain, blood vessels, joints and every other part of the body. A sedentary lifestyle is a direct route to an earlier death. Inactivity kills us—*literally.*

Just how does physical exercise help us live longer and better?

Here are some of the ways:

- Exercise helps you FEEL GOOD! Life becomes more fun, and the *high* that comes from exercise won't let you down later. Moreover, the hormones producing the exercise high are proving to be health promoting as well.

- Exercise strengthens the heart. This is important in a culture in which every second person dies of heart and vascular disease.

- Exercise lowers blood pressure and resting heart rate, protecting the heart and blood vessels.

- Exercise lowers LDL cholesterol levels in the blood and often raises HDL cholesterol, again decreasing heart and vascular risk. (LDL is the bad part of cholesterol; HDL is the good part.)

- Exercise strengthens bones by helping retain calcium and other important minerals. Sedentary people past age forty increasingly lose calcium and bone mass.

- Exercise lifts depression. Outdoor exercise is one of the most valuable tools for fighting this common and disabling malady.

- Exercise relieves anxiety and stress. In our harried, pressured society, physical activity is proving to be an effective antidote.

- Exercise increases overall energy and efficiency in all areas of our lives.

- Exercise helps maintain desirable weight levels. It builds muscles and burns fat. Moderate exercise blunts appetite by temporarily increasing blood sugar levels.

- Exercise improves circulation, and that makes for clearer minds, better sleep and faster healing of damaged body areas.

What kind of exercise are you talking about? Not everyone can jog or run marathons.

Every one of these listed benefits can come from plain, simple walking. Walking is the ideal exercise. It is inexpensive; it is safe. Nearly everyone can do it. And it is fun! You can select your own speed and stop when you want. As your fitness improves, you can gradually add speed and time.

Other good exercises are swimming, bicycling, gardening, yard work and golf—if you leave the carts behind. For hardier souls, jogging, stair climbing, rock climbing, jumping rope and snow skiing provide challenging variations. In bad weather, try stationary bicycles, trampolines, rowing machines or simply walking or jogging in place. To be effective, active (aerobic) exercise should be brisk and continuous for at least twenty minutes. Most people can work up to this goal. A daily program of thirty to forty minutes of active exercise will give you maximum benefits. To control weight, increase the time to one hour. You can divide the hour into two or three sessions if you wish.

Is it true that reaching a certain pulse rate is necessary for exercise to be effective?

There are exercise regimens for specific purposes. The concept of *training heart rate* is particularly useful in strengthening the heart. Weight training is also proving valuable. But remember: Even moderate activities, such as brisk walking, will improve fitness and lower the risk of heart attack as much as 30 percent. Every step counts.

But I hate to exercise. It's boring!

We all do many boring things every day: brushing teeth, cleaning the house, washing the car, mowing the lawn, doing dishes, going to work. But we do these things because we like the rewards: beautiful teeth, an attractive home, a clean car, a regular paycheck. After awhile these activities become routine, an accepted part of our daily living.

Let's look at exercise the same way. Its benefits are far greater than a clean house—they will last a lifetime.

My level of fitness?

How would you rate your level of fitness?

___ High: I have a regular exercise program.

___ Medium: Sometimes I exercise, but not regularly.

___ Low: I don't exercise; I rest.

There has to be an easy way.

Have you tried exercise before and found that you just couldn't stick with it? If so, you should try the world's easiest exercise system. It's called the *Ten-Step Exercise Program.*

All you do is make a commitment to the first ten steps of a daily walk. That's it. You get out and take those steps every day. Once they're behind you, you can turn around and go home if you wish.

The system works because it eases you past those difficult first steps. It gets you up and going, and if you are like most people, once you get going, you will finish the entire walk.

Another reason the *Ten-Step Exercise Program* is valuable is that it keeps you in the habit of exercising even when you can't manage your full routine. You might be sick or traveling, yet in almost every situation you can manage ten steps. In this way you maintain the exercise habit even when you can't exercise. That's important if you want to enjoy the benefits of fitness for the rest of your life.

Anything else?

Another useful technique is to plan your exercise sessions in advance. Make an appointment with yourself for at least thirty minutes—longer if you are exercising to lose weight. If you are an early riser, try exercising before breakfast. If your morning is already too full, walk during your lunch hour or in the evening. The important thing is to find a time that is right for you.

Also, to liven up your sessions, include friends and family members in your exercise activities. If they won't join you, take the dog out for a stroll. Exercise can be enjoyable if you approach it with an attitude of fun and creativity.

CHAPTER SUMMARY

Exercise slows down the aging process. It strengthens the heart, lowers blood pressure, relieves stress, eases depression and helps you maintain a desirable weight. You don't need expensive equipment or a health club membership to start. Walking can provide all these benefits and more.

An Assignment

Schedule your exercise sessions in advance, and use the *Ten-Step Exercise Program* to get you moving. Regular exercise is as necessary as air, water and wholesome food. Don't let another week go by without it.

The No-Calorie
Wonder

Forcing the body to work with limited amounts of fluid is like trying to wash the dinner dishes in a cupful of water. When you don't drink enough water, the body must excrete wastes in a much more concentrated form, causing body odor, bad breath and unpleasant-smelling urine.

Don't most people drink plenty of water?

Surprisingly, the average person today drinks more soft drinks and alcohol than water. And not far behind the preferred drinks are coffee and milk.

Notice what happens next time you go to a restaurant for a meal. Even if you are served a large glass of ice water, the waiter will probably ask you expectantly, "And what would you like to drink?"

Why does it matter what beverages I drink? They all contain water, don't they?

The body uses water in all forms, but beverages can pose special problems. Many have calories that must be digested like food. These calories may produce extra fat storage, swings in blood sugar and slowed digestion. Water alone, on the other hand, goes right through the stomach whether or not food is there. It requires no processing, no digesting, does not irritate or disturb body functions, and it has no calories.

Sugar in beverages requires extra water for metabolism. Most beverages increase acid secretion in the stomach. Cola drinks contain phosphorus, a chemical that can help deplete the body's calcium supplies, contributing to brittle bones.

Do the "no sugar" diet drinks solve the problems?

Diet beverages don't contain sugar, but they present other concerns. Nearly all beverages, sugared or not, contain chemicals that are added for color, flavor, preservation and other reasons. Some of these may irritate delicate stomach linings, and some may also require the liver and kidneys to detoxify and dispose of them.

Drinking *water* eliminates these problems. There are no extra calories to slow down digestion or add unwanted fat, no irritants to stress sensitive linings of the digestive tract, and fewer foreign chemicals to threaten delicate body machinery.

How much water should I drink?

Enough to keep the urine pale. The body loses about ten to twelve cups of water a day through the skin, lungs, urine and feces. Food provides two to four cups of water, leaving us six to eight glasses of water to drink for adequate hydration.

Get into the habit of drinking water liberally. Drink on arising, in mid-morning, mid-afternoon and early evening. A drink of water is like an internal shower—it rinses the stomach and prepares it for its work.

So start the day right. Give that early morning drink some zest by adding a twist of lemon. Then during morning and afternoon *coffee breaks,* reach for a glass of water and drink until your body's content. In the evening, drink away some of your sleepiness and the temptation to snack.

Water is exactly what the body needs to carry out all its life processes. It is the perfect beverage, and one of life's greatest blessings.

The next time you are asked, "Anything to drink?" you can say, "Yes, a glass of water is fine. In fact, it's perfect."

Eight glasses—that's a lot!

Sandy had made up her mind. She was going to give her body the water it needed: eight glasses a day, without fail. Opening the cupboard, she selected a large tumbler. This, she decided, would be her glass.

Things didn't go well for Sandy that day. Eight glasses turned out to be a lot of water. When she wasn't sipping, she was scurrying down the hall to the bathroom.

No wonder people don't drink enough water, thought Sandy. *I feel like a sponge.*

Sandy was making things difficult for herself. If she had taken time to measure, she would have found that the glass she had selected held 16 ounces of liquid—two cups of water. Instead of drinking the eight 8-ounce glasses recommended, she was drinking twice that amount.

Sandy switched to a smaller cup. Now she gets the water she needs without wearing a path to the bathroom.

I know I should drink more water, but it's hard.

Water really is the most healthful drink. We can live only a few days without it. Even though we all get enough to sustain us, most people don't drink enough for optimum functioning. We sip enough to survive, when we should be drinking enough to thrive. The result is unnecessary stress placed on the body's cleansing system and other functions.

One way to make sure you get your daily quota is by drinking two glasses of water when you wake up in the morning. Do this before you get caught up in the activities of the day. With two glasses down, you only need to drink four to six more during the rest of the day. That is a feat everyone can manage.

But I'm not always thirsty.

Are there other times in the day when it would be convenient for you to take a water break? If you wait until you are thirsty, you probably won't get enough.

In the spaces below, list times when it would be convenient for you to stop and have a drink. Once you make these pauses a habit, your body will always have the fluid it needs.

_____

_____

Chapter Summary

Today, North Americans drink more soft drinks and alcoholic beverages than water. These liquid substitutes force the body to deal with calories and chemicals, and they can disturb the process of digestion. The body needs water to function properly. When you want refreshment, choose the real thing—water.

An Assignment

Drink six to eight glasses of water each day this week, but make sure the glasses are the right size. An 8-ounce glass (one cup) is recommended. Be good to yourself: Start enjoying nature's super fluid today.

Designer Water

With reports of contamination by heavy metals, nuclear wastes, fertilizers, pesticides, herbicides and leaking fuels—not to mention the sorry state of some public water supply systems—some people are afraid to drink the water that comes out of their kitchen faucet.

What are some alternatives to tap water?

Fortunately, there are reasonable alternatives to drinking water with questionable quality, though the following cautions are given for your consideration:

- *Bulk waters* sold in one-gallon plastic jugs are the most popular. These come from springs or wells, or are processed from ordinary tap water.

- *Mineral waters* contain dissolved minerals, sometimes natural, sometimes added. There are no upper limits set for the amount of minerals that can be put in.

- *Sparkling water* is a generic term for any carbonated water. Some, like club sodas, are relatively high in sodium and should not be used by people with high blood pressure.

- *Seltzer water* refers to filtered, carbonated tap water that has no added mineral salts. Many, however, have added sugars, up to 100 calories per 8 ounces.

- *Distilled water* is the purest. All minerals have been removed, either by distillation or by osmosis, leaving the water tasting rather flat. It is the hardness of the water—the minerals—that give water its flavor.

Is bottled water safer or better tasting than water from the tap?

A lot of people must think so. Last year Americans spent more than $1 billion on bottled waters!

You should know, however, that federal and state requirements for bottled water are exactly the same as they are for tap water. If your water supply is up to standard, what comes out of your faucet may be just as pure, just as safe and just as wholesome as the water you buy in a grocery store.

As a matter of fact, according to several research centers, most of the ordinary tap water sampled in North America proved to be as good or better than most bottled waters.

Are you saying that most tap water is safe to drink?

It is true that some water supplies have been chemically contaminated. It is also true that outbreaks of infectious diseases have been traced to tap water—though this is extremely rare in developed countries today. But we need to keep this in perspective. Many people fear flying, even though statistics show that they are safer in an airplane than in a bus, train, automobile or even crossing a street. Likewise, any problem with a water supply is apt to be broadcast out of all proportion to the real danger it poses to the majority of people.

How can I tell if my tap water is safe?

There are a number of ways to protect yourself:

- Public water systems are checked for safety, sometimes several times a day. The test results are public property, and you can request a copy.

- If you suspect possible contamination between your

municipal supply and your home, you should have your water tested at the point of its use.

- If you are among the 40 percent of Americans who depend on private wells, your local government may test your water for a nominal fee. National mail order testing services are also available.

What can I do if my tap water is unsafe?

If you live in an area with unsafe water, you can protect yourself by installing your own filtering system. (An under-the-counter device may be all you need.) A good charcoal filter removes most contaminants and makes the water taste good. Other more sophisticated methods are also available.

There are simpler solutions as well. The dangers of lead poisoning can be minimized by running the tap for a minute or so before drinking from it. As for chlorine, draw water into an open pitcher or a glass jar and let it stand. The chlorine will evaporate, and the taste will improve.

This all seems so complicated. No wonder some people fear their drinking water!

The irony is that most of us face more health hazards from not drinking enough water than we do from its possible contaminants. Tap water is hundreds of times cheaper than bottled, and it is nearly always at our fingertips. If it checks out safe, we should not fear drinking it. Just make sure to drink plenty of it—six to eight glasses a day.

While it is true that we can't protect ourselves from every conceivable danger, there is much we can do. Heart disease strikes every other person in the United States. Cancer and diabetes afflict millions more. Lack of exercise makes most of us old before our time. It is with these dangers that we should concern ourselves most.

- What makes more sense, reinforcing your roof against the one-in-a-billion chance that a passing airplane may drop a frozen sewage bomb, or starting a regular exercise program?

- What makes more sense, eating fruits and vegetables needed for good health, or avoiding them on the off chance that they may contain pesticide residue?

- What makes more sense, drinking the eight glasses of water that your body needs to flush out toxins, or avoiding tap water for fear that it may contain something dangerous?

A healthy body provides good insurance against the dangers that we may face. The body's ability to heal and protect itself is truly remarkable.

CHAPTER SUMMARY

In most cases, the health hazards we face from not drinking enough water are greater than those from possible contaminants in the water supply. If you are concerned, have your water tested, or install a good charcoal filter. A filter helps purify your water and makes it taste better.

AN ASSIGNMENT

Before you let a headline panic you, make sure you know how serious a threat is involved. Take action if warranted; otherwise, relax in the knowledge that your new lifestyle is boosting your body's ability to protect itself.

Kiss of the Sun

E xcessive exposure to sunlight can cause skin cancer as well as premature wrinkling and aging of the skin. In proper amounts, however, the sun's rays can be good for your health.

You say "proper amounts." Can sunlight be measured?

Yes. It is important to understand the power of sunlight. Most of us have observed how dim even the brightest electric light bulb appears in daylight. The intensity of light is measured in "lux," or "luxes." For example, outdoor light can reach 3,000 lux on a bright sunny day. A bright indoor environment may provide only 400 lux, less than 15 percent of daylight brightness.

In recent years, melatonin, a natural body hormone, has been found to enhance sleep. Melatonin levels reach a peak in children and fall slowly and steadily throughout adult life. This may explain why children sleep so much better than older people.

The body carefully regulates melatonin production. The process is largely controlled by the light-dark cycle. Optimal melatonin production occurs only at night, in a dark environment. The pineal gland, located in the center of the brain, is the "clock" that regulates this process at the right time.

Melatonin is not stored in the body. We need a liberal supply each evening to sleep well. Studies demonstrate that daily exposure to natural sunlight will boost melatonin output. Artificial light is a weak substitute, as are manufactured supplements.

What are some of the good things about sunlight?

A lot!

Sunlight is an efficient germ killer. That is why it is important to sun and air out blankets, quilts and other items that are not washed regularly and sterilized in an automatic dryer.

Proper amounts of sunshine also give the skin a healthy glow and help make it smooth and pliable. A moderately tanned skin is more resistant to infections and sunburns than untanned skin.

Also, sunlight elevates the mood for most people, producing a sense of well-being. (Just don't stay out too long and get sunburned!) Combined with active exercise, sunshine is an important adjunct in treating acute and chronic depression. Remember, when depressed during winter's cold and gloomy months, try to catch any possible ray of sunshine.

What's more, the body is able to manufacture vitamin D by the action of sunlight on the skin. Vitamin D enables the body to pick up calcium from the intestines for use in building healthy bones. It prevents both childhood and adult rickets and aids in the prevention of osteoporosis.

Sunlight also helps to:

- Enhance the immune system.

- Alleviate pain from swollen arthritic joints.

- Relieve certain symptoms of PMS.

Some reports suggest that sunlight may also help lower blood cholesterol levels.

And the bad things about the sun?

Sunlight is a major risk factor for skin cancer, especially in light-skinned people. Too much sunlight, for them, may be particularly damaging.

You should also know that burning the skin is extremely harmful for everyone. Every burn destroys healthy, living tissue. Repeated burns cause irreversible damage and can set up a person for skin cancer.

And if all that isn't bad enough, repeated sunburn and even repeated deep tanning of the skin gradually destroy its elasticity and its oil glands, producing wrinkling and premature aging.

Some recent studies suggest that a high-fat diet, when combined with exposure to sunlight, may also promote skin cancer.

What are some guidelines for safe, healthy exposure to sunlight?

- Modest tanning is protective, like putting sunglasses on your skin. But you must understand your own tolerance to sunlight. Fair-skinned people and redheads may have to begin with only five minutes of exposure to the sun per day. Darker-skinned people can begin with ten to fifteen minutes per day. Up to thirty minutes of sunshine, exposed to as much of the body as possible, is a realistic goal for most people.

- Never, never burn! Wear protective clothing, eyewear and a protective sunscreen if needed. Be especially careful around snow or water and on cloudy days.

- If you have an outdoor trip or vacation coming up, prepare your skin by giving it progressive exposure in the days beforehand, to the point of "pinking up."

- A few minutes of sunshine on your face and hands each day will produce all the vitamin D you need.

- Open up your house to the sunshine each morning. It will improve your health and lift your spirits.

For thousands of years, sunlight has been known as a mediator of life. But we know today that it can be healing or destructive; it can be the kiss of life or the kiss of death, depending on how we use it.

How much time in the sun is good?

How often do you spend time in the sunshine?

__ Every day, weather permitting

__ Most days

__ A few times a week

__ Rarely

It is good to spend at least a few minutes in the sunshine every day. Studies have shown that, for some people, lack of exposure to light may cause depression. For everyone, taking a sunshine break gives your body a dose of vitamin D and acts as a disinfectant, killing bacteria on your clothes and skin.

During the summer do you:

__ Sizzle and sunburn?

__ Work on a deep, dark tan?

__ Tan lightly?

__ Stay out of the sun completely?

If you sizzle and burn or go for that deep tan, watch out! You are putting yourself at risk for skin cancer and damaging the elasticity of your skin.

On the other hand, lightly tanned skin is more resistant to sunburn and less prone to infection. Get outside in the fresh air. Soak up a little sunshine each day, just don't overdo it.

When it is bright outside, do you open up your curtains and let the sun into your home?

__ Always

__ Sometimes

__ Never

Open up your windows and let the sunshine in. It will kill germs, lift your spirits and enhance your health. Carefully consider the "sunlight suggestions" in the following chart.

Sunlight Suggestions

1. Avoid going to sleep in the sun. It is a recipe for a severe sunburn.

2. Use sunscreen and sunglasses to protect yourself. A hat is also helpful to shade your face when you are working outdoors.

3. Be extra careful when you are around water or on snow. The reflection from these surfaces can increase your exposure, causing you to burn rapidly.

4. If you are swimming, remember to reapply your sunscreen when you are finished. Better yet, use waterproof sunscreen.

CHAPTER SUMMARY

Sunshine can be good for you. It kills germs, helps improve your mood and allows the body to produce vitamin D. Yet, while some exposure is good, too much can destroy the skin's elasticity and increase the risk of skin cancer. Enjoy sunlight and outside activities, but protect yourself from overexposure.

AN ASSIGNMENT

Get some sunshine every day. Combined with exercise in the fresh air, sunlight is one of nature's most effective remedies.

Deadliest Drug in the World

S moking is not only hazardous to your health—it can be hazardous to your job prospects as well. Twice as many smokers are out of work as nonsmokers. Though few will admit it, most employers would reject a smoker competing for a job with an equally qualified non-smoker.

Don't you think the risks of smoking are being exaggerated?

The hard facts consistently point to tobacco as the deadliest drug in the world. Last year it killed 468,000 Americans—more than all who died from AIDS, street drugs, fires, car crashes and homicides combined. It also kills thousands more *involuntary smokers*—persons forced to breathe *secondhand* smoke.

How does smoking cause lung cancer?

Normally your lungs' air passages are lined with millions of tiny hairs called cilia. The cilia act like little brooms, protecting the air tubes by sweeping dusts, tar and other foreign materials gradually upward, like escalators, until they can be spit out.

Every time a blast of tobacco smoke hits these cilia, however, they slow down and soon stop moving. As a result, the trapped tars from the tobacco smoke begin boring into the cells lining the air tubes. Over time, this constant irritation turns some of the cells cancerous.

This transformation takes many years. But once it begins, the cancer steadily eats its way deeper into the lung. By the time it is discovered, it is usually too late.

Is lung cancer the leading cause of death in smokers?

No. Tobacco causes 128,000 lung cancer deaths per year in the United States alone. Close to 90 percent could have been prevented if the people had not smoked.

The nicotine and carbon monoxide in tobacco smoke are the main culprits that promote vascular disease. While nicotine produces the sensation of soothing relaxation and well-being—the main appeal of smoking—it also constricts small arteries, depriving the heart, brain, lungs and other important areas of vital oxygen. Nicotine is also addictive.

Carbon monoxide interferes directly with the ability of red blood cells to carry oxygen. This causes shortness of breath and lack of endurance. It also promotes and accelerates atherosclerosis, the narrowing and hardening of the arteries.

That's a lot of bad news. Is that all?

Unfortunately, there is a lot more.

- Smokers have much more cancer of the mouth, larynx, esophagus, pancreas, bladder, kidneys and cervix than do nonsmokers.

- Emphysema and bronchitis gradually destroy lung tissue, producing death by suffocation. In the United States, 60,000 of these grisly deaths occur each year as a result of smoking.

- Smokers have two to three times the risk of stomach and duodenal ulcers than nonsmokers.

- Smoking pulls calcium out of the skeleton, accelerating the bone-thinning process known as osteoporosis.

- Smoking during pregnancy has been linked to increased risks of tubal pregnancy, low birth weight babies, still births, sudden infant death (SIDS), respiratory infections, malformations and decreased IQ by an average of 9 points.

If a person has smoked heavily for a long time, does it pay to quit?

Smokers who quit begin to heal almost immediately. As the nicotine and carbon monoxide leave the body, the smoking-related risk for heart disease decreases dramatically. Although the risk for cancer decreases more slowly, the danger lessens as the weeks and months go by.

There are other payoffs to quitting: a sense of victory, increased self-esteem, pleasant breath, better-tasting food, increased endurance, improved health and energy, a feeling of well-being and freedom from an inconvenient, unpopular, costly habit. Quitting may also open the way to more job opportunities.

Americans often overreact to the most trivial of risks while ignoring much more substantial threats to their health and safety. For example, at least 25 percent of all smokers die prematurely from some disease connected with their habit, losing an average of twenty-one years of life. And yet many people react more forcefully to evidence of a one-in-a-million risk of getting cancer from chemicals found in drinking water!

It is time to get life back into perspective. The biggest favor you can do for your body is to kick the habit and freely breathe clean air again. Listen to instruction from the Bible:

> Do you not know that your body is a temple?…
> Therefore honor God with your body.
> —1 CORINTHIANS 6:19–20, NIV

How can I kick the habit?

The first step in breaking any habit is to decide that you are going to change. It is not enough just to want to change or to imagine that you will change someday. Breaking an addiction to tobacco requires positive commitment.

What are the pros and cons?

When making a life-changing decision, it helps to look at the pros and cons of the situation. There actually are some reasons to continue smoking.

Reasons to Keep Using Tobacco

1. Tobacco gives a pleasurable sensation of soothing relaxation and well-being.

2. Tobacco suppresses the appetite, making it easier to keep excess weight off.

3. Quitting can be a disruptive, uncomfortable and stressful process.

4. Lighting up is a good excuse to take a break.

5. Trying to quit, and failing, hurts the smoker's self-esteem.

These are some pretty powerful reasons to keep smoking, especially when combined with physical and psychological addiction to nicotine. Anyone who faces these issues and overcomes them deserves respect and admiration.

While there are some reasons to keep smoking, there are far more persuasive reasons to stop—reasons that convince thousands to quit each year.

Reasons to Quit Smoking

1. Quitting is the single most important thing you can do for your health and longevity.

2. Quitting will reduce the risk of heart disease, stroke and cancer of the lungs, mouth, throat, pancreas, bladder, kidneys and cervix.

3. Quitting reduces risk of emphysema and osteoporosis.

4. Quitting eliminates the risk posed to the smoker's family from secondhand smoke.

5. Quitting lessens the chance of a smoker's children and grandchildren smoking.

6. Quitting will give you better breath, whiter teeth and fewer wrinkles.

7. Quitting means less time spent sick and more physical endurance.

8. Quitting will lower medical and insurance costs.

The list goes on, and it grows longer every year as we learn more about the harmful effects of tobacco.

If you smoke, what will it take for you to quit? If you don't smoke, what was it that kept you from starting or helped you give it up?

_____

_____

_____

CHAPTER SUMMARY

Tobacco is the deadliest drug in the world. In the United States alone it kills over 450,000 people a year. Close to 90 percent of lung cancers could be prevented if people stopped smoking. The biggest favor people can do for themselves is to break the smoking habit.

AN ASSIGNMENT

If you smoke, get information about the different methods of breaking the habit. Choose your method, set your goal—then do it! Some can quit cold turkey; others will need to seek help in a stop-smoking program.

The Cooler
Delusion

They look like soft drinks, taste like soft drinks and are sold like soft drinks. But there the similarity stops. These drinks contain more alcohol than a beer or a glass of wine, and they carry more calories.

Are you talking about wine coolers? They look so attractive, so healthy!

That is the selling strategy. Coolers come in a rainbow of colors that people associate with fruit juices. In fact, the containers and carrying packs are often plastered with pictures of fresh fruit, even though some contain no fruit or fruit juice at all.

What's more, coolers taste sweet and fizzy, like soft drinks. The alcohol taste is disguised, making them attractive to people who do not ordinarily drink alcohol. Then, too, coolers are not packaged like other types of alcoholic beverages, but like soft drinks.

Do coolers carry less risk than other alcoholic beverages?

The worst part of the cooler caper is the illusion that coolers are low in alcohol. They're not. Coolers average 6 percent alcohol by volume, whereas a beer averages 4 percent.

And because coolers typically come in 12-ounce bottles, the amount of alcohol in a serving can exceed that of a gin and tonic (with

1 ounce of liquor) or a glass of wine served at dinner.

How are coolers affecting today's young people?

Teens, especially teenage girls, are attracted to coolers. They like the name, which suggests a light, refreshing drink. And they like the taste. "Coolers are a hazard for kids because they're so easy to drink," says Diane Purcell of Chicago's Parkside Medical Services. "You can go from lemonade to a lemon cooler in one easy step. You don't have to acquire a taste for alcohol."

How serious is alcohol use among teens?

While statistical data varies from study to study, it is clear from all that many children as young as sixth graders have tried wine coolers. Junior and senior high schoolers admit to using alcohol, and many have serious problems stemming from alcohol use.

Are these kids in danger of becoming adult alcoholics?

Many kids are already alcoholics by the time they reach adulthood. Others are well on their way. When it comes to alcohol, youth carry their habits into adult life. And there are already 10.5 million adult alcoholics. Half of all fatal auto accidents involve alcohol, as do a growing number of air fatalities. Unless we can help our teenagers, things aren't going to get better.

Alcohol exacts a heavy price from personal health. Alcohol promotes high blood pressure and is directly toxic to heart muscle. Alcohol increases the risk of stroke, sudden death from heart arrhythmias and diseased heart muscle, congestive heart failure, cirrhosis and cancer. Alcohol also increases morbidity and hospitalization and reduces the drinker's years of useful life. And it ravages the lives of family and friends.

Perhaps the saddest statistics to emerge in recent years are those of damaged babies who are permanently retarded due to their parents' alcohol use.

What can be done to protect our young people?

Wine coolers are big business. They account, then, for a significant amount of the industry's sales—a cool $1.7 billion. Their attractiveness could be limited if coolers—

- Were clearly labeled as alcoholic beverages, not for sale to anyone under twenty-one.

- Had large warning labels attached about the health hazards associated with drinking alcoholic beverages.

- Were subject to extra taxes, thus adding another small barrier to their availability.

And most important of all, young people who grow up in *nonalcoholic homes* are statistically less inclined to have problems when they reach adulthood. There is no influence more powerful than that of a good parental example. Consider this advice:

> Wine is a mocker and beer a brawler; whoever is led astray by them is not wise.
>
> —PROVERBS 20:1, NIV

What about my drinking habits?

If you drink, it can be helpful to review your drinking habits periodically. The following questions are designed to bring your current habits into focus.

Evaluating My Drinking Habits

1. In what situations do you use alcohol?

___ Never, I don't drink
___ To unwind after work
___ At social gatherings
___ On special occasions: birthdays, anniversaries
___ With meals at restaurants
___ At taverns or bars

2. How often do you drink alcohol?

___ Never, I don't drink   ___ Several times a week
___ A few times a year   ___ On weekends
___ A few times a month   ___ Every day

3. When you drink, how much do you consume at one sitting?

__ 1 drink   __ 3 or 4 drinks
__ 2 drinks   __ 5 or more

Are you satisfied?

How satisfied are you with your answers? Do they represent the
behaviors you value? If not, what could you change?

How many calories?

Throughout this book we have urged you to avoid highly refined
products that are high in calories but low in nutrition. Alcohol certainly falls into this category. Two cans of beer, for example, carry 300
calories; two jiggers of 100 proof whiskey, 250 calories; two glasses of
dessert wine pack 280 calories—and they are all empty calories, providing none of the nutrients your body requires.

Altogether, alcohol accounts for 9 percent of the calories in the
American diet. No wonder we are overfed and undernourished.

CHAPTER SUMMARY

Alcohol extracts a heavy price from personal health. This goes for teens
as well as adults. Young people who grow up in nonalcoholic homes are
less likely to have problems with alcohol when they reach adulthood. A
parent's example can make a big difference.

AN ASSIGNMENT

Make this "ban the booze" week at your house. You should be able to
get through it without any sort of urge or discomfort.

If you can't, you need to seriously consider who is the master: you or
the alcohol. If you can get through the week with no problems, why not
quit altogether? It will help keep your weight under control, improve
your nutrition and set a good example for the young people in your life.

Wired!

E very day eight out of ten North Americans take a psychotropic (mind-stimulating) drug. The culprit? It is everyday, ordinary, over-the-counter caffeine.

How can that be? Explain.

Do you know many people who don't drink at least one cup of coffee a day? Or tea? Or take an *extra-strength* pain reliever? Or guzzle down a soda? Although caffeine-free sodas are available, they are favored mainly for children and people with medical problems that are affected by caffeine.

But I need a lift now and then! And caffeine isn't *addictive,* is it?

An addictive substance produces observable and measurable physical and mental effects when it is withdrawn. In this sense, even small doses of caffeine, taken regularly over time, will usually produce some degree of addiction.

A good way to check yourself is to stop all caffeine intake for a few days. The most common physical withdrawal symptom is headache, varying from mild to severe. Sometimes a migraine is triggered. Other physical manifestations include feelings of exhaustion, lack of appetite, nausea and vomiting. Symptoms last one to five days.

Psychological withdrawal can be even harder. Depression may occur. People become accustomed to reaching for the *pick-me-up* throughout the day. The urge can be compared to the desire for a cigarette—it may be difficult to resist.

Does caffeine damage the body?

These are definite known negative effects on the body caused by consumption of caffeine:

- Most obvious is an overstimulated nervous system with tremors, nervousness, anxiety and problems with sleep. In time, these symptoms give way to chronic fatigue, lack of energy and persistent insomnia.

- Caffeinated beverages can cause stomach irritation. While additives are primarily responsible for this effect, caffeine itself has a constricting effect on blood vessels. It can thus interfere with digestion. High doses of caffeine induce vomiting.

- Caffeinated drinks also stimulate the stomach to excrete excessive acid, producing a rebound effect. This aggravates ulcers and other stomach problems.

- Caffeine has been found to interfere with calcium and iron absorption. With increasing concern over osteoporosis and anemia, these are factors to consider.

- Caffeine raises blood sugar levels, which, along with its mind-stimulating action, produces increased energy. While this seems desirable, the increased blood sugar level draws out an insulin response, which not only cancels the surge, but also produces a letdown. This letdown triggers the "yo-yo" syndrome—reaching for another caffeinated drink, and then another, and yet another.

- Caffeine irritates the kidneys, causing diuresis (increased urine output). Some studies have linked cancers of the urinary tract to caffeine use. Caffeine has been also shown to precipitate asthmatic attacks and stir up allergies.

Are there some healthful alternatives to the caffeine high?

Yes, here are a few energy-boosting suggestions:

- When you get up in the morning, follow your hot shower with a blast of cold water and towel off briskly.

- At work, stand up, stretch and take a few deep breaths every hour or so.

- Take a brisk walk at break time or during lunch hour.

- Drink a cup of cold (or hot) water several times a day.

- Rub a coworker's back and ask for a return favor.

- Walk to a window and relax your eyes on the distant landscape.

- Tidy up your work area.

All these good things will make you feel better. Look for other creative ways to get a lift without the predictable letdown caffeine causes.

What about coffee?

Imagine going to buy coffee at the grocery store and finding the coffee section missing.

"What's going on?" you ask the clerk. "Where is the coffee?"

"Oh, haven't you heard? Coffee has been classified as a drug. The pharmacist sells it now."

Shaking your head in disbelief, you walk across the store to where the pharmacist dispenses medications, drugs and—caffeinated beverages.

The pharmacist smiles at you knowingly. "You look like you're here for some coffee. I can tell from your expression."

You nod and tell him what brand you would like.

"That's fine," he says. "No prescription necessary—I just need to type up the warning label."

"Warning label?"

"That's right. Just the usual. It says 'Warning: This drink contains caffeine. Possible side effects include addiction, tremors, nervousness, anxiety, insomnia, chronic fatigue, lack of energy, stomach irritation, vomiting, interference with calcium and iron absorption, and the aggravation of ulcers.'"

He hands you the coffee, but you decline. "No thanks," you say. "I think I've changed my mind."

Are You an Addict?

You could be a caffeine addict without even knowing it. Here are some questions and a suggestion to help you find out.

On a weekly basis, do you frequently consume any of the following?

___ Coffee
___ Tea (exclude herbal teas)
___ Chocolate
___ Caffeinated soft drinks

How important is a cup of coffee in the morning?

___ Essential: can't get going without it.
___ Important: helps jump-start the day.
___ Enjoyable: it's pleasant once in a while.
___ What is coffee? I never touch the stuff.

Suggestion:

One way to find out if you are addicted is to stop all caffeine intake for a week. If you're hooked, chances are good that you will notice physical symptoms like headache, lack of appetite, and nausea, which can last from one to five days. Psychologically, you may feel down and listless, and of course, there will be a strong urge for your favorite beverage.

How can I break the habit?

If you find you're a "caffeine fiend," here are a few things you can do to ease through withdrawal:

1. Drink plenty of fresh water.
2. Slow down your daily activities.
3. Exercise in the fresh air.
4. Get the support of others around you.
5. Reward yourself for taking such a positive step.

In a crisis, would just a little caffeine really matter?

Occasional small doses of caffeine will hardly make a difference. The trouble is, most of us have a hard time knowing when to stop.

Chapter Summary

Caffeine is an addictive drug. It produces physical and mental effects when withdrawn. While an occasional small dose of caffeine may not make a difference, heavier use has been linked to health problems.

An Assignment

Skip the caffeinated drinks like tea, coffee and soda for a while. See how you fare. Then review this material and give serious consideration to making your body a caffeine-free zone.

Spiders and Sledgehammers

The way some people use drugs makes no more sense than using a sledgehammer to kill a spider. Most people don't realize that common, over-the-counter drugs can have unpleasant—even dangerous—side effects.

You must be exaggerating.

I wish I were! Take something as common as aspirin, for instance. Many people down it at the least sign of a headache, flu or fever. Every twenty-four hours, as a matter of fact, Americans consume over forty tons of this drug!

Aspirin is known to promote stomach ulcers and has been associated with Reye's syndrome, an often fatal disease in children.

Acetaminophen, another common painkiller, can cause skin rashes and even—in extreme cases—kidney and liver damage.

But prescription drugs are safe when you follow directions, right?

In the medical world, new and more effective wonder drugs are being discovered and introduced almost daily, while older ones are improved and refined. Yet the *perfect drug* still eludes us—the one that will do its job with absolutely no deleterious side effects.

Consider blood pressure drugs, for example. They are the most widely used prescription medications on the market and among the most effective. Yet they carry a host of side effects, which can include weakness, fatigue, drowsiness, headache, mental depression, dizziness, bloating, sweating, indigestion, unstable emotional states, slurred speech, raised cholesterol levels and impotence. People who need these drugs often must test several different kinds before they find one they can tolerate.

The point is, no drug is completely safe. Even life-saving antibiotics carry potential problems such as nausea, vomiting, diarrhea and allergic reactions.

Why then are people so anxious to take drugs?

While most of today's diseases respond to lifestyle measures (such as a better diet and regular exercise), doctors who advocate these principles often find themselves rowing upstream. People are impatient; they want quick fixes rather than real solutions. If one doctor doesn't produce the desired prescription, they often seek another who will.

Simply put, people today too often want to believe there is a magic potion for their particular problem. We have developed an almost childlike faith that drugs can help us pep up, calm down, regulate weight and ward off almost every conceivable ailment.

So why risk taking any drug?

Anyone taking a drug must always balance *risk* against *need*. If you have a serious bacterial infection, for instance, the risk you run by taking an antibiotic is outweighed by the risk you run if you don't take it.

If you have a tension headache, on the other hand, you would probably be better off taking a brisk walk or a nap.

What are some guidelines for using drugs intelligently?

A good rule of thumb is to reserve drugs for specific, identifiable needs that can't be met by lesser measures. Don't use a *big-gun* medicine like antibiotics, for instance, for a *flyswatter* problem like a head cold.

Likewise, a warm bath or a cup of herbal tea is better than a sleeping pill if you can't get to sleep. And if you don't *want* to go to sleep, a cold shower or a brisk walk is better for you than a *wake-up* pill.

When you *do* take a drug, be sure you know exactly what it is supposed to do. Understand its risks and side effects, how and when to take it, and the signs of overdose. Don't mix medicines, and don't risk psychological dependence or physical addiction by taking any drug longer than needed. If you have more than one doctor, make sure your main doctor knows all the medications you are taking.

In short, give drugs the respect they deserve. Save them for times when they are truly needed. It is time to stop hitting spiders with sledgehammers.

Can't I take something for pain?

Too many people run to the medicine cabinet whenever they feel the slightest ache or pain. They don't realize that pain often acts as a warning system, telling us something is wrong.

We may be eating too much, drinking too much, smoking too much or taking on obligations beyond our capacities. When pain is blocked by drugs, we ignore these causes rather than changing the behaviors that cause the pain in the first place. This kind of neglect sets the stage for more serious diseases.

We have suggested that drugs are divided into two categories: those that attack the cause of the problem and those that help relieve symptoms.

If you take any medications, list them in the spaces below. Write a "C" next to those that attack the cause of the problem. Put an "S" by those that simply help relieve symptoms.

The Drug Checklist

Before you take any drug, there are a few things you should find out:

1. Is the drug absolutely necessary?

2. Will the drug conflict with other medications you are already taking?

3. Exactly how long will you need to take the drug?

4. What are the possible risks and side effects associated with the drug? (No medication is completely safe. Even aspirin can have side effects.)

5. Is there a non-drug alternative? (Many problems can be controlled by lifestyle measures.)

6. Is addiction possible with this drug? (Drugs prescribed for pain, anxiety or sleep disorders are habit forming.)

What if I do have to take a drug?

When you need to take a drug, here are some things to keep in mind.

1. Don't quit taking it unless you get approval from your physician. Many drugs need to be taken for a certain period of time. Quitting early can render the treatment ineffective.

2. Don't take a larger dosage than you are prescribed. It is not true that if a little of something is good, more is better. In fact, more can be deadly. Take your medications only as directed.

3. Let your doctor know that you would prefer not to take drugs if possible.

CHAPTER SUMMARY

Many people have a childlike faith in drugs and medicines. They take them for every conceivable ailment. But using big-gun medicines for flyswatter problems or for problems that should be solved by lifestyle measures can leave you tired, depleted and depressed. Use drugs sparingly and with care.

AN ASSIGNMENT

Don't go running to the medicine cabinet for every little ache and pain. The cure is often worse than the problem. When you must take a drug, be sure you get the answers to the questions on the drug checklist.

When Breathing
May Be Hazardous

Houseplants do a lot more than enhance the appearance of our homes and offices. They enrich the air with oxygen and absorb carbon dioxide; some even remove toxic pollutants from the air we breathe.

You mean harmful pollutants can collect indoors?

Increasingly so. Many modern homes and office buildings are tightly sealed to save energy costs. But this advantage may be offset by poor ventilation and potential accumulation of indoor air pollutants.

Tobacco smoke, of course, is the most dangerous pollutant, but there are others.

Formaldehyde, for example, seeps from certain wood products, and other chemical fumes come from carpeting, copy machines, upholstery, cleaning products and freshly dry-cleaned clothes. Carbon monoxide and nitrogen dioxide, two poisonous gases, may come from gas, oil and coal furnaces, gas ranges, fireplaces and kerosene heaters.

Other problems occur from dust, air mites, molds and fungi, ozone, lead, asbestos, pesticide residues and, in some areas, radon gas.

How do these pollutants affect people?

Symptoms range from burning eyes, sore throats, coughing and itching to headaches, sluggishness, nausea, dizziness, feelings of exhaustion and depression. This cluster of symptoms is sometimes referred to as "sick building syndrome."

What is the best way to protect ourselves?

First, we can *control exposure.* For example:

- Ban smoking indoors. Even secondhand smoke contains hundreds of harmful chemicals.

- Make sure all gas, oil and kerosene and coal-burning heaters and appliances are properly vented to the outdoors, as well as coal and wood-burning furnaces and fireplaces. And don't forget gas cooking ranges and clothes dryers.

- Keep heating and air-conditioning units well maintained. Clean air ducts and filters regularly.

- Keep chimneys open and in good repair.

- Use air fresheners, moth crystals, etc., sparingly.

- Avoid idling a vehicle in an attached garage or near an open window.

Are there other things we can do?

The most obvious solution to indoor pollution problems is to *improve ventilation.* Open windows and set up good cross ventilation. Fresh air not only dilutes trapped fumes, thus decreasing their health threats, but it enriches stale air as well. People often don't realize that in closed areas the same air can be breathed and rebreathed, over and over. The oxygen content decreases, and the carbon dioxide and other wastes increase, resulting in sleepiness, sluggishness and headaches.

Here are some suggestions:

- Set air conditioners and heating systems to bring in 20–35 percent (or more) fresh air. Energy costs will be somewhat higher, but health benefits will more than compensate for this.

- Air out your house at least once a day. On smoggy days, air out the house at night or in the early mornings. In most areas smog particulate matter drops considerably once the sun has set.

- Sleep with an open window. Set up cross ventilation in your bedroom if possible. You'll wake up feeling refreshed.

What about air-cleaning machines?

These machines can be expensive, complicated and messy, and most have a limited range. However, people with allergies and certain lung ailments often find them helpful. And we recommend them for anyone exposed to air polluted with tobacco smoke at home or at work.

How does air relate to personal health?

Air is composed of about 20 percent oxygen, the rest being nitrogen along with a few other gases. Since the human body operates on oxygen, each one of its one hundred trillion cells must receive steady, fresh supplies, or die. Oxygen is picked up in the lungs from the air we breathe and delivered to our bodies via the red blood cells. Well-oxygenated cells are healthy and contribute to overall well-being. Anything that diminishes oxygen supplies to the lungs or its delivery to body cells is detrimental.

Air molecules can also be positively or negatively charged. Polluted air is usually full of positive ions. It is commonly found on freeways, at airports and in closed, poorly ventilated areas.

Air containing an abundance of negative ions is plentiful around lakes, in forests, near rivers and waterfalls, at the seashore and after a rain storm. This kind of air is refreshing and gives people a lift.

Another "feel good" technique is to stop where you are and take a few slow, deep breaths several times a day. This gives your body an extra "shot of oxygen" and helps unload carbon dioxide.

Yet another way to flush your body with oxygen is to exercise. Activity opens up blood vessels and speeds those oxygen-laden red blood cells on their rounds.

And remember the houseplants. Placing at least one plant for every 100 square feet of indoor space is recommended. Live plants not only "eat" many toxic pollutants and freshen the air with oxygen; they probably slip in some extra negative ions as well!

Right now, without changing anything about the way you are sitting or breathing, answer the following questions:

Air Inventory

1. How are you sitting right now? Is your spine straight, or are you slouching? Are your shoulders rolled forward?

2. Observe your breathing for a few moments. Is it shallow or deep?

3. Do the clothes you are wearing or the chair you are sitting in restrict your breathing?

4. Is the room you are in well ventilated with fresh air, or is it closed and stuffy?

5. Is there cigarette smoke or heavy smog in the air?

6. Have you (or will you) exercise today?

7. Have you eaten a high-fat meal today? (A high-fat meal reduces your blood's ability to carry oxygen.)

8. When was the last time you got up and moved around? Have you taken a break or done some deep breathing during the last couple hours?

I've heard breathing exercises are good for you.

Take a moment to try this simple breathing exercise. It will energize and refresh you.

Stand or sit with your back straight. Exhale deeply through your mouth. Now, draw the air back into your lungs. As you do, imagine it going right down into your belly, filling it. Feel your stomach expand as you inhale.

When your lungs are full, slowly begin to exhale. Tighten the muscles of your stomach as you gently push the last bit of air out.

Repeat the process, slowly, five or six times.

Do this exercise when you wake in the morning and several times during the day. If possible, step outdoors into the fresh air. Refresh body and mind by giving yourself a caffeine-free boost.

CHAPTER SUMMARY

Oxygen is vital to each of the trillions of cells that make up your body. Poor breathing habits or poor air can rob the body of this vital element. Bad air and poor breathing habits promote negative emotions like depression and irritability. It can also cause headaches and chronic feelings of fatigue and exhaustion. Make sure you get enough oxygen by exercising, keeping your house well ventilated and pausing frequently to take slow, deep breaths.

AN ASSIGNMENT

Practice breathing deeply, and experiment with the other tips listed in this chapter.

CHAPTER 51

How Much Is Enough?

Life today is fast paced, exciting—and exhausting. Insomnia is epidemic. People are gulping down millions of sedatives and tranquilizers, desperate for rest that will restore their energy.

Why am I always tired?

You may have an illness, such as a cold or the flu, that is sapping your energy. Or you may be depressed.

Many otherwise healthy people, however, work in confining sedentary jobs with deadline pressures and emotionally draining problems. These people are not likely to feel rested when they get out of bed in the morning.

In addition, few people get through a day anymore without a pick-me-up, usually coffee, tea or soda. Caffeine is a central nervous system stimulant and a common cause of insomnia.

What about chronic fatigue?

Besides tiredness and a lack of energy, there is also an increase in irritability. Tempers get short, and patience goes out the window. Everything requires more effort, until finally the simplest tasks seem overwhelming.

Fatigue also sabotages creativity. Judgment suffers and efficiency goes. And if unrelieved, fatigue can culminate in exhaustion and full-scale depression.

How does rest relate to these problems?

It is important to understand the function of adequate rest for our bodies. Here are a few of the vital processes affected by proper rest:

- Rest allows your body to renew itself. Waste products are removed, repairs are effected, enzymes are replenished, and energy is restored.

- Rest aids in the healing of injuries, infections and other assaults on your body, including stress and emotional traumas.

- Rest strengthens your body's immune system, helping to protect you from disease.

- Proper rest can add length to your life. In a large population study of health habits a few years ago, it was found that people who regularly slept seven to eight hours each night had lower death rates than those who averaged either less than seven hours or who slept longer.

How much rest do I need?

People need different kinds of rest. A relaxing night's sleep is a good start. Newborn babies sleep from sixteen to twenty hours, while young children need ten to twelve hours. Adults vary widely in their requirements, but most do best on seven to eight hours per night.

People also need a change of pace. During World War II, Great Britain instituted a seventy-four-hour work week but soon found that people could not maintain the pace. After experimenting, they found that a forty-eight-hour work week with regular breaks, plus one day of rest each week, resulted in maximum efficiency.

Society also recognizes the need for other breaks from time to time. The long weekend is now an American institution, and yearly vacations have proven their value.

What about sleep medications? Are they helpful?

During normal sleep the body passes back and forth between

periods of light and deep sleep. During light sleep dreaming occurs; this apparently provides a natural outlet for the pressures and tensions that build up during the day.

Medicated sleep, however, while producing a welcome state of unconsciousness, suppresses that dream stage. And even though people believe they have slept soundly, they may not feel as refreshed and energetic the next day.

Sleep medications may be helpful in emergencies, but they will contribute to chronic fatigue if continued over time.

Alcohol is another commonly used drug that seems to produce relaxation and aid sleep. But alcohol-induced sleep is not as restorative as normal sleep.

How can I sleep better?

Many seemingly unrelated, simple activities can help you to sleep better. Here are some of them:

- Take frequent breaks during the workday. Walk around, get a drink of water, take some deep breaths.

- Daily engage in thirty to sixty minutes of active exercise. Exercise relaxes, restores energy, helps banish depression and combats nervous tension.

- Maintain as regular a schedule as possible for going to bed, getting up, eating and exercising. The body flourishes on regular rhythms.

- Eat the evening meal at least four hours before bedtime. An empty, resting stomach is more conducive to quality rest.

- Try a lukewarm (not a hot) bath. It is a helpful relaxation technique.

- Count your blessings. Fill the mind with gratitude and thanksgiving.

Rest is an important part of life's rhythm. And like a dancer, if we go with our rhythms, we will be in tune with ourselves.

What if I'm still tired?

Feeling tired? Have a hard time getting out of bed in the morning?

The following questions are designed to get you thinking about your sleep habits.

Sleep Quiz

1. I have trouble falling asleep at night.

a. Usually   c. Rarely
b. Often   d. Never

2. I get enough sleep and awake feeling rested.

a. Usually   c. Rarely
b. Often   d. Never

3. I use caffeinated drinks (like coffee and soft drinks).

a. More than 10 cups/day
b. 5–9 cups/day
c. 2–4 cups/day
d. Less than 2 cups/day

4. I go to bed at night early enough to get a good night's sleep.

a. Always   c. Rarely
b. Often   d. Never

I have trouble falling asleep. Do you have any suggestions?

Many people occasionally have trouble falling asleep. Three common reasons are emotional stress, caffeine consumption and lack of exercise. Fortunately, all of these can be controlled.

Caffeine, found in coffee, tea and many soft drinks, can be reduced or eliminated from the diet.

Emotional stress can also be reduced by handling disturbing problems earlier in the day, when you are rested. Don't wait until bedtime to bring up problems to your spouse, for example.

A regular exercise program may be the best medicine of all for ensuring a good night's rest. It reduces stress and provides a pleasant physical fatigue that helps you sleep soundly.

For many, getting to sleep isn't the problem—making time for it is. Busy schedules, bolstered by strong coffee, cut into the hours needed for sleep.

Your body is your most valuable possession. It may be tempting to skip sleep, but in the long run that is counterproductive. A parable by Stephen Covey from his book *The Seven Habits of Highly Effective People* illustrates this point:

> Imagine you are walking through the woods and you come upon a man feverishly trying to saw down a tree. The man looks exhausted. He says he has been sawing on the same tree for five hours.
>
> "Why don't you take a break for a couple minutes and sharpen that saw?" you ask. "It will cut faster."
>
> "No time for that," he gasps. "I'm too busy sawing."

CHAPTER SUMMARY

Rest is an important part of life's rhythm. Most adults do best with seven to eight hours of sleep each night. If you have trouble sleeping, don't reach for sleep medications. Take a warm, relaxing bath. Exercise daily. Maintain a regular schedule. Strive for a clear conscience and tranquil mind.

AN ASSIGNMENT

Sharpen your saw by allowing yourself enough time to rest. Set a regular time to wake up, and go to bed early enough to get seven or eight hours of sleep. If you do, you'll find that you are able to accomplish more during your waking hours.

Living the
Ultimate Life

I s this all there is?" sighs the aging baby boomer, surrounded by his very considerable possessions. Having bought into the "grab all you can get" philosophy of the 1980s, he has every material thing his heart desires. Yet, he feels curiously empty—and disappointed.

Isn't that a common human problem?

Yes, and it is getting worse. Americans are living longer, healthier lives than ever before, yet surveys show that they feel less and less satisfied.

Our hopes are continually being inflated by grandiose and unrealistic advertising, self-help gurus who promise the moon, and our childlike faith in medicine's ability to cure all our ills. As disappointments pile up, we shuffle along, looking for the missing pieces of our lives.

Are people ever really satisfied?

Early on we dream of wealth, fame and success, of having what we want and doing as we please. But can you think of a multimillionaire athlete who isn't itching for a bigger contract? Or a wealthy celebrity who hasn't felt drawn to do yet another commercial, endorse a bigger product or produce a new book? Where is the businessman who wouldn't jump at the next big deal or lust after another merger?

On another level, do you know a teenager who is satisfied with his or her looks? Clothes? Friends? On the face of it, humans appear to be creatures of insatiable desires.

Is this why so many people turn to drugs?

In today's fast-paced life, people often feel so pressured and stressed, so full of pain and disappointment, and so hopeless, that they become increasingly willing to gamble their health and even their lives on almost anything that promises relief, no matter how temporary. "Follow your feelings," they are urged. "If it feels good, do it." "Hurry, life is passing you by."

For every skid row bum there are scores of closet alcoholics. And for every street punk looking for a hit, there are many so-called respectable people numbing their pain with prescription pills.

But lasting joy doesn't come in snorts, or well-being from bottles and pills. You can't shoot up peace of mind. Gratitude and compassion aren't sold in the drugstore or on the street.

So how does one go about getting joy, peace—those good things?

The Bible says that following our "fleshly" or "natural feelings" leads to negative results like immorality, debauchery, selfish ambition, drunken orgies and fits of rage. (See Galatians 5:19–22, NIV.)

The Bible also says that God wants better things for us, such as peace, joy and healing. (See Romans 10:17; 3 John 2.) These gifts, however, come through the cultivation of our spiritual nature.

Is that kind of religious mumbo jumbo relevant for today?

It is right on. Look at alcoholism, for instance. The medical miracles and the technological advances of the past half century have hardly touched this disease. Alcoholics Anonymous (AA) continues to offer the most consistently effective treatment with the best long-term results. AA uses a twelve-step program that involves a recognition of human helplessness and the acceptance of a Higher Power. Similar twelve-step programs, based on the philosophy of AA, are proliferating in almost every area of human need. They are bringing healing to thousands for whom medical care, drugs, counseling and other human solutions failed.

This decade is witnessing a renewed search for values, a resurgence of faith and an increasing acceptance not only of a Higher Power but of a personal, caring God.

Could this be just another fad?

This *fad* has strong roots in reality—and in history. One of the most exciting breakthroughs in recent years has been the discovery of the strong and close relationship of the physical, mental, emotional and spiritual components of human beings.

This is a radical departure from the past because for centuries it was believed that body, mind and spirit were separate entities that functioned independently of each other.

Now we're discovering that things like anger, fear, resentment and distrust can actually produce effects on the body that weaken its immune system and open the door to disease. Conversely, positive emotions like love, joy, faith and trust produce protective substances that strengthen the immune system and protect the body from disease. Harboring bitterness and hatred, nurturing negative thoughts and feelings can make us sick; cherishing positive thoughts and feelings can make us well—literally.

What does "spiritual growth" involve?

It could involve getting acquainted with your Bible, worshiping and singing praise songs with other believers and praying for the special "fruit of the Spirit" that God wants you to possess—love, joy, peace, patience, kindness, gentleness, self-control. (See Galatians 5:22–23, NIV.)

Where do you turn for renewal? What is at your core, your center of being? The testimony of our history is clear: Those who were most content in life drew strength and renewal from a Source larger than themselves. They perceived the touch of the infinite in the beauty of nature, the wisdom of the Scriptures and the private stillness of meditation and prayer.

The spiritual dimension of life is an area about which science has little to say. Yet poets, wise men and our own hearts affirm its importance.

We are fearfully and wonderfully made. (See Psalm 139:14.) We don't arrive in this world, as some evolutionists claim, with only the minimal equipment needed for survival. We are each given a conscience to keep us on track, a full range of feelings and emotions to enrich our lives, and a brain that we can never use up or wear out.

What is this spiritual dimension?

Health and fitness are not enough, neither are wealth, fame, good looks or power. The Ultimate Lifestyle includes the dimension of spiritual growth and development. It brings a contentment in which we learn that if we are not satisfied with what we have, we will never be satisfied with what we want.

Let those deep, inexplicable longings lead you to the One who can give your life hope and meaning—God. Spiritual growth supplies the missing pieces and fills the empty spaces. The result is a life of quality and fulfillment that will stretch into eternity.

How can I attain this spiritual dimension?

Like all things of value, cultivating the spiritual side of our nature takes an investment of time. Attention must be shifted from immediate concerns to deeper, eternal issues. We need to take time for stillness, away from the commotion and noise of our everyday lives.

We need time to explore the deeper side of ourselves, to read inspiring words or just to walk in the sunshine and fresh air.

When was the last time you allowed yourself to really enjoy the people closest to you? How long has it been since you joined with others who find faith and inspiration in seeking relationship with God? What are some things you could do to enhance your spiritual life?

CHAPTER SUMMARY

The ultimate lifestyle includes not just health and fitness, but also spiritual growth. Trust in God supplies a missing piece in our lives. It brings quality, fulfillment and hope for the future.

AN ASSIGNMENT

This week take some time to step back and think about what is truly important to you. Look beyond the clamor of daily activity to the universal themes of life. Choose to read the Bible along with another inspiring book; listen to some uplifting music. Give thanks to God for His marvelous gift of life and health. Every breath you take is a miracle, and every morning is a new start.

Summary

To win the battle against the epidemic of Western lifestyle diseases, we must break with the lethal excesses of today's Western diet. We need a simpler, more natural way to eat.

As incredible as it might seem, there is *one* diet that not only prevents most of these killer diseases, but also helps reverse them.

Such a diet consists of a wide variety of foods eaten *as grown,* simply prepared with sparing use of fats, oils, sugars and salt. It contains very few refined, engineered products. Animal foods, if used, are strictly limited.

Adopting this simpler, more natural dietary lifestyle brings improved health and increased energy. We can eat larger quantities of food without gaining weight, and still cut our grocery bills in half. Where, indeed, can we find a better bargain than that?

Comparison		
	U.S. Diet	**The Optimal Diet**
Fats and oils	35-40%*	15%*
Protein	14–18%*	10–12%*
Sugar/day	35 tsp.	under 10 tsp.
Cholesterol/day	400 mg	< 50 mg
Salt/day	12–15 gm	< 5 gm
Fiber/day	10 gm	> 30 gm
Water (fluids)/day	minimal	8 glasses

*of total calories

Basic Guidelines for a Lifetime of Good Eating

U se the following "Eat Less" and "Eat More" charts to give you an "at-a-glance" manual for healthy eating.

EAT LESS

Visible fats and oils

Avoid fatty meats. Strictly limit cooking and salad oils, sauces, dressings and shortening. Use margarine and nuts very sparingly. Avoid frying; sauté instead with a little water in non-stick pans.

Sugars

Limit sugar, honey, molasses, syrups, pies, cakes, pastries, candy, cookies, soft drinks and sugar-rich desserts—like pudding and ice cream. Save these foods for special occasions.

Foods containing cholesterol

Avoid meat, sausages, egg yolks and liver. Limit dairy products, if used, to low-fat cheeses and nonfat milk products. If you insist on eating fish and poultry, please use sparingly.

Salt

Use minimal salt during cooking. Banish the salt shaker. Strictly limit highly salted products like pickles, crackers, soy sauce, salted popcorn, nuts, chips, pretzels and garlic salt.

Alcohol

Avoid alcohol in all forms, as well as caffeinated beverages such as coffee, sodas and black tea.

EAT MORE

Whole grains

Freely use brown rice, millet, barley, corn, wheat and rye. Also eat freely of whole-grain products, such as breads, pastas, shredded wheat and tortillas.

Tubers and legumes

Freely use all kinds of white potatoes, sweet potatoes and yams (without high-fat toppings). Enjoy peas, lentils, chickpeas and beans of every kind.

Fruits and vegetables

Eat several fresh, whole fruits every day. Limit fiber-poor fruit juices and fruits canned in syrup. Eat a variety of vegetables daily. Enjoy fresh salads with low-calorie, low-salt dressings.

Water

Drink six to eight glasses of water a day. Vary the routine with a twist of lemon and occasional herb teas.

Hearty breakfasts

Enjoy hot, multigrain cereals, fresh fruit and whole-wheat toast. Jump-start your day.

Basic Guidelines for a Lifetime of Healthful Living

N E W S T A R T®

NUTRITION

- Nourish your body with healthful, full-fiber, nutrient-rich foods.
- Increasingly, move toward a totally vegetarian lifestyle.
- Enhance digestion by breaking the snack habit.

EXERCISE

- Strengthen your body and increase your enjoyment of life with daily active exercise, outdoors if possible. Aim for at least thirty minutes a day. Walking is the safest exercise and one of the best.

WATER

- Come alive with an alternating hot and cold shower in the morning.
- Rinse out and refresh your insides, too, by drinking six to eight glasses of water each day.

Sunshine

- Pull back the drapes! Let the sunshine in! It will lift your spirits, brighten your day and improve your health!

Temperance

- Live a balanced life. Make time for work, play, rest and hobbies. Nurture relationships and spiritual growth.

- Protect your body from harmful substances, such as tobacco, alcohol, caffeine and most drugs.

Air

- Air out your house daily. Sleep in a room with good ventilation.

- Give your body a shot of oxygen by taking frequent deep breaths. Walk outdoors every day.

Rest

- Aim for seven to eight hours of sleep a night. Go to bed early enough to wake up feeling refreshed.

- Devote time to a change of pace. Attend church, go on a picnic, plant a garden, pursue a hobby, take relaxing, enjoyable vacations.

Trust

- A life of quality and fulfillment includes spiritual growth and development.

- Love, faith, trust and hope are health-enhancing. And they bring rewards that endure.

This material is a registered trademark of the Weimar Lifestyle Program. It is based on eight health principles: Nutrition, Exercise, Water, Sunshine, Temperance, Air, Rest and Trust. Used by permission of Weimar Institute, Weimar, California 95736.

The NEWSTART acronym is a registered trademark of the Weimar Lifestyle Program, Weimar, CA 95736. Used by permission.

Bibliography

Barnard, Neal, MD. *Breaking the Food Seduction*. New York: St. Martin's Press, 2003.

———. *Eat Right, Live Longer*. New York: Harmony Books, 1995.

Fraser, Gary E., MD, PhD. *Diet, Life Expectancy, and Chronic Disease*. New York: Oxford University Press, 2003.

McDougall, John, MD. *The McDougall Program*. New York: Plume Books, 1991.

Melina, Vesanta, RD, Brenda Davis, RD and Victoria Harrison, RD. *Becoming Vegetarian*. Summertown, TN: Book Publishing Company, 1995.

Messina, Virginia, RD, and Mark Messina, PhD. *The Vegetarian Way*. New York: Crown Trade Paperbacks, 1996.

Nedley, Neil, MD. *Proof Positive*. Ardmore, OK: Neal Nedley Publ., 1999.

Nestle, Marion, PhD. *Food Politics*. Berkeley, CA: University of Berkeley Press, 2002.

Physicians Committee for Responsible Medicine. *Healthy Eating for Life Series*. New York: John Wiley & Sons, 2000–2002.

Robbins, John. *Diet for a New America*. Walpole, NH: Stillpoint Publishing, 1987.

———. *The Food Revolution: How Your Diet Can Help Save Your Life and Our World*. Conari Press, 2001.

Schlosser, Eric. *Fast Food Nation*. New York: Houghton Mifflin Company, 2002.

Thomas-Peters, Cheryl, RD, and James A. Peters, MD, DrPH, RD. *More Choices Cookbook*. Hagerstown, MD: Review and Herald Publ. Assn., 2003.

RESOURCES FOR YOUR HEALTH

OK. You've made the decision to start living more healthfully. But how? Fortunately, there is plenty of information out there, but unfortunately, it is all too confusing! So where do you go?

For straight answers to important questions on health, the Lifestyle Medicine Institute, directed by Dr. Hans Diehl, world authority on lifestyle medicine issues, has produced three great ways to start your health program:

Better Health—New Beginnings

This comprehensive three-video set (six hours) will teach you how to eat more and weigh less; reduce your cholesterol; reverse diabetes, high blood pressure and heart disease; and live longer without getting older. In four weeks your life will be changed forever. Call or write for more information.

More Choices Cookbook by Cheryl Thomas-Peters, RD and James A. Peters, MD, DrPH, RD

Simple solutions to eating well. Enjoy healthy, great-tasting meals in minutes! One hundred fifty savory, slimming, professionally developed recipes and a patient-proven plan help you achieve your ideal weight and optimal health. Spiral, 144 pages.

More Choices Cookbook also features:

- Kitchen-tested recipes including: breakfast, lunch, dinner and special occasions to make meal planning simple
- Incredible color photography
- Nutritional analysis
- Diabetic exchanges
- Menu-planning tips
- Shopping guide
- Spiral-bound book

Lifeline Health Letter

This 24-page quarterly newsletter, edited by Dr. Hans Diehl, features cutting-edge information on lifestyle health issues—inspirational and reinforcing—a perfect companion for those who are serious about lifestyle change. Ask for a free sample copy. Call or write for more information.

Better Health Productions
P. O. Box 1761
Loma Linda, CA 92354
Phone: (909) 825-1888

Visit us online at
www.BetterHealthProductions.com